Suffer the rains to dissolve in the fiery sunlight,
and purified reascending heavenward bear my cause,
suffer a friend to grieve I perished so soon
and on fine evenings, when someone prays in my memory,
pray also, O my Land, that in God I repose.

Pray for all who have fallen befriended by no fate,
for all who braved the bearing of torments all bearing past,
for our pitiful mothers, piteously breathing forth bitterness;
for orphans and widows, for those in tortured captivity
and yourself - pray to behold your redemption at last.

And when in dark night shrouded the graveyard lies
and only, only the dead keep vigil the night through,
keep holy the peace, keep holy the mystery.
Strains, perhaps, you will hear - of zither, or of psalter:
it is I: O Land I love: it is I who sing to you!

And when my grave stands wholly remembered
and unlocated (no cross upon it, no stone there plain)
let the site be wrecked by the plow and cracked by the spade,
and let my ashes, before they vanish to nothing,
as dust be formed a part of your carpet again.

Nothing then will it matter to place me in oblivion -
across your air, your space, your valleys shall pass my wraith,
A pure chord, strong and resonant, shall I be in yours ears:
fragrance, light, and colour - whisper, lyric, and sigh,
constantly repeating the essence of my faith.

Land that I idolize, prime sorrow among my sorrows,
beloved Filipinas: hear me the parting word.
I bequeath you everything - my family, my affections.
I go where flourish no slaves, no butchers, no oppressors,
where faith doesn't kill: where God's the sovereign Lord.

Farewell, my parents, my brothers - fragm
friends of old and playmates in childhood
offer thanks that I rest from the restless day
Farewell, sweet foreigner, my darling, my delight!
Creatures I love - farewell! To die is to repose.

Jose Rizal
Translated by Nick Joaquin

PHILIPPINES

archipelago of smiles

PHILIPPINES
archipelago of smiles

Duly accredited by the National Centennial Commission

Preface by N.V.M. Gonzalez, National Artist

Part one
Unusual Philippines
Nine reportages by Eric Pasquier

Part two
"Bayan Natin" Our Country
by a team of Filipino Writers and Academics
under the direction of N.V.M. Gonzalez

le cherche midi éditeur • **Paris** • **S.O.S Incorporated** • **Manila**

Preface

by N.V.M. Gonzalez

Born in Romblon, in 1915, N.V.M. Gonzalez grew up in Mindoro and began writing after high school. Among his earliest poems was "Notations", which appeared in Poetry: a Magazine of Verse, edited by Harriet Monroe. His first collection, Seven Hills Away, a gathering of short stories about Mindoro originally published in the Philippine Magazine, and late in 1947 by Alan Swallow, won him a fellowship to Stanford University and identified him as the first Filipino writer to appear on the post-World War II literary scene.

Other books followed, including A Season of Grace (novel), Children of the Ash-Covered Loam and Other Stories, and Selected Stories. In 1960, he was awarded the Philippine Republic Cultural Heritage Award for Literature, and that same year the Jose Rizal Pro-Patria Award for The Bamboo Dancers.

His teaching career included professorships at the University of the Philippines, California State University (Hayward), University of Washington and University of California (Berkeley and Los Angeles).

In 1987, the University of the Philippines conferred upon him the degree of Doctor of Humane Letters (honoris causa), for "shaping the Filipino short story and the novel, for making a new clearing within the English idiom and tradition on which he established an authentic vocabulary." Two other collections of short fictions followed: Mindoro and Beyond (1992), and The Bread of Salt and Other Stories (1993), and later the essays gathered in 1996 under the title Work on the Mountain. A novel of his early period, The Winds of April, was reissued by the University of the Philippines Press, even as under the auspices of the Manila Literary Circle, his latest book, The Novel of Justice, received the 1997 National Book Award for the Essay. Among the books launched at the 1997 Philippine Book Fair was A Grammar of Dreams and Others Stories, his most recent collection of stories. He is currently Writer-in-Residence at the University of the Philippines.

In recognition of his contributions to the national and international artistic community, and for his "tireless dedication, patience, sensitivity and unflagging interest in the development of the literature and languages of the Philippine", he was recently conferred the title of National Artist for literature.

Our story begins with Alexandre Dumas, author of The Thousand-and-One Phantoms, which had quite a following in Manila. Among its readers was a single-minded and rather venturesome young man named Paul Proust de la Geroniere of Nantes, who had founded a colony in Laguna Province, in a place called Jala-Jala. He had indeed set up himself there for keeps, collecting taxes, fighting skirmishes with the banditti, and keeping the peace. He liked hunting wild buffaloes and crocodiles, and drinking dreadful-looking wine with Tinguians. That the man was mad was an impression held by the many who admired him; for his part, he had a feeling though that M. Dumas, out in Paris, took him for a phantom like a character in the popular fiction.

But Jala-Jala was for real, M. de la Geroniere had created an Eden out of the jungle. He had courted and posted a rich Creole widow, the Marquesa de las Salinas, as mistress at his domain. Perhaps their life could project an aristocracy on the rise, even as Fortune was already smiling upon their efforts. "I was really in existence," wrote M. de la Geroniere, lest Jala-Jala persisted as fiction. "I resolved (then) to take up the pen, under an impression that facts of the most scrupulous veracity, and which can be attested to by hundreds of persons, might possess some interest.

Today's politics of globalization could not have been even a mote in the imagination when M. de la Geroniere wrote his Twenty Years in the Philippines; but we are especially fortunate on account of the authentic treasure throve of information that the book offers our age. About Filipino behavior today much is available from M. de la Geroniere. The economic and social order deep down has scarcely changed. He found datuism workable and could get things done; Jala-jala became a productive farming community. He introduced and perfected the culture of coffee, winning recognition for the enterprise from the Spanish government even as his own government accorded him the decoration of the Legion of Honor.

We still have the coffee. The hacienda, which has been apparently with us all these years, appears to be on the decline, though not the tradition of "noble and generous hospitality" of the countryside that it nurtured. Self-esteem and, arguably, a warm response to technology and global political and economic forces were to come as well. A nation was in the making and a people conscious of its birthrights would not be short changed. Filipinos seemed destined to deal with the coming century with hope and confidence.

What now lies ahead for him? Let Eric Pasquier help out with some answers. These photographs are a harvest of many visits. The scenes belong to both the camera and the viewer. Let him be grounded on the basic country facts which the catch of essays gathered here provides. Thereafter, it will be discovered that the camera has rendered each scene with a pride of place that they have in fact quietly shared together.

History means remembering the past in a systematic and fundamentally significant way through language, and it might as well be that only glimpses of it seem possible at any one time. Silvino V. Epistola's "Into the Light of History" provides us one such momentary view of what once caused us to squint in the sun: remember how readily Filipinos were associated with the Chinese. This has claimed several pages in the earliest Sino-Philippine chronicles.

In the community of nations then known, the Philippines were, in a manner of speaking, pearls, corals, sea shells, betel nut, ginger, and wax. In turn, the natives of our islands wanted pottery, lead, colored beads, and, last but not least, gold. A sophisticated system of exchange allowed merchants to use certificates in lieu of money. Many a coconut tree at some seaside grove must have afforded welcome shade to visiting traders as well as the local crowd even as, from afar, with the sound of the surf in their ears, more outriggers approached with fresh stocks of turtle shells, bamboo and rattan baskets.

But who were the people that Chinese traded with? Wasn't it a wonder that they were that ready for maritime commerce? They were land- and sea-dwellers, procurers of barter-worthy hemp to the last hank and pearls of the most delicate sparkle. Here was a people destined to prosper, and they did. In their languages are imbricated values that tell us how successive colonizations would not obliterate them. Prospero R. Covar offers us a portrait, using clues from Tagalog to help explain how to this day the Filipino is literally held together by language and the folkways they derive from it.

As late as this age, the Tagalog language has yet to become, along with other vernaculars, a steady base to serve the demands of orality and popular entertainment. The development of a national language, to be called Filipino is something in the nature of a dream constantly on the verge of being diminished and eventually erased by the popular idiom. While one does not wish this to happen at all, there is the entertainment and information of the West, already riding the global media highways. It is probably impossible to dam up this flood at any point. Within the country, the Filipino himself is learning skills in this area even as he adapts the received language to his needs and makes it a vehicle for serious imaginative work. It is probably safe to say that in the immediate future the more significant contributions by Philippine thought to world culture will become available through English rather than any other language.

For now, though, one is sometimes tempted to describe the dislocations of today, the failure to obey routine traffic regulations or the observance of common courtesy and decency in dealing with one's fellows, for example, as breaches of behavior attributable to the fractured language situation, hence also a fractured view and experience. When advocates of nationalism urge students to go Filipino but exhort them to patriotism in English, there is an inherent weakness in the sentiment, a superficiality in the rhetoric, a clue to the all-too-generic blandness of patriotic ideas. While Philippine languages, of which there are at least twenty-one, draw from a common source, as Dr. Covar's essay suggests, a nationwide word list understandable to a large portion of the population awaits to be evolved. Meanwhile this has enabled the Filipino, using English for his language of global culture, to remain in good standing and keep his stall.

One is reminded of how Latin once took over wherever Catholicism held sway so that eventually it became the language of a universal church. The lesson is relevant to any study of "progress." That the Filipino has a commitment to "progress" has been well enough demonstrated early on. His native languages survived in spite of both Spanish and English. Now, the very facility and range achieved by later generations of writers in English, particularly after World War II, have all the more enhanced the appreciation on a worldwide scale of how far the country has moved forward over the years.

His first challenge had involved syllabic script writing. It was said to have been introduced in the country during the 11th century, the only surviving samples being those presently used by ethnic groups in Palawan and Mindoro. They have remained very much the ethnographic curiosities that they are. When exposed to the earliest efforts of the xylographic press even as the Spanish clergy promoted Catholicism, Philippine society buttered up a sizable educatable class, allowing it to move grudgingly up the social scale. There soon appeared on the scene such pioneers as Tomas Pinpin, in the art of printing, and such harbingers of a literary culture in the person of ladinos, pages or servants, invariably members of the literati coopted by the establishment "to entertain guests, execute lively songs and dances, and to sing profane and unmodest songs," to quote from a document of 1598 by the redoubtable apologist and historian Antonio de Morga.

The point to underscore here is that the Filipino comes across with surprises. In due course, from obscure and unpromising beginnings could come, and they did, poets like Jose de la Cruz (Huseng Sisiw, 1746-1829) and Francisco Baltazar (Balagtas, 1788-1862); eventually, from no tradition to speak of in scholarship and the composition of serious and extensive long works, would evolve Jose Rizal (1961-1996). Spanish led Filipino intelligence and imagination toward schools of new ideas. The language of command became transformed into one for illumination. Spanish was not colonialism's gift as much as it was that of the modern world's, and soon enough it became the vehicle of a people's long repressed will to freedom and its articulation in the field of action. Rizal warned against haste, but here was a time too decisive for comfort.

But the Revolution did not turn out as successfully as envisioned; other forces were engulfing the nation. The fires set ablaze in the countryside by Andres Bonifacio and Emilio Aguinaldo take on now, in retrospect, the familiarity of a classic scenario while further efforts towards economic and cultural freedom became imperative, self-generated and assertive. Before the banquet, the pomp and banderetas at Malolos had been the French-style revolution that Filipinos only all-too-readily wanted to learn from and apply. As an effort by a people adept at gestures, the follow-through had to materialize decades later at Edsa.

In the current financial crisis that the world, and our part of Asia appears to be weathering through, national leadership keeps reminding us about the strength of the fundamentals under which our politics and economics work. Well and good, says the man in the street. The future is beyond enthusiasm but equally beyond despair as well. The Filipino will come through: bahala na ! Is the formula that his vernacular experience supplies, with religions, animism, and superstition in addition coming further to his aid. Uncertainty may be relied up to be consistent, and no one is truly any worse for it. Hindsight now helps him see that Rizal's sojourn as a medical student in Europe had not changed him as a Filipino as much as it defined his very citizenship in an as yet-to-be-founded republic inspired deeply by French ideals.

Whatever it is that Philippine society might be honored for today did not accrue by chance: some factors had been allied with the people, generally kindly as Nature has been. The three colonizations and a homegrown dictatorship did not get exacerbated by vile weather but by a single-mindedness before which the Filipino response was not stubborn enough. Surprisingly enough, despite *this inadequacy, he managed to prevail. One explanation if explanations are in order at all - is that he enjoys access to those aforesaid vocabularies, two ways of naming Reality and understanding, albeit in his own manner, and in what appears to be his own style.*

These vocabularies supply him with what might be called the identifiable realities of his experience. Each vocabulary represents one world where his "at home-ness" is predicated. This condition, a duality perhaps uniquely Filipino, is his good fortune: there is the native or vernacular vocabulary on the one hand, and on the other, the received or learned word lists that colonial experience left behind. It is no surprise then, when closely observed, that he will be seen to feel comfortable with both.

The story of the Filipino effort over time, and the forces regnant in that cultural and material marketplace, have been given a shrewd accounting in Juan T. Gatbonton's essay. As a Southeast Asian journalist with Hong Kong for his base and Manila as a vacation resort, as it were, he developed an interest in the politics and economics in the Region rare for his generation. It is particularly helpful to observe that while the political and social problems of the Philippines today may draw from the pre and post Marcos years immunerable supportive histories, they are scarcely singular in significance. Manila, Cebu, and other centers of trade and cultural life have their counterparts elsewhere, and more readily identifiably so, in Southeast Asia; but with one difference. The country has a more Western look, which Hong Kong, Seoul, or Djakarta do not have. The streets are as grimy as those of Bangkok or Calcutta; but there is dirt and filth of what might be called a Manila category, triumphant and defying description. Numbers come to one's aid, but in due course one's sensibilities surrender in defeat.

Is the all-too-fragile peso a symbol of that feeling? To which word list does the exchange slump belong? Yet Mr. Gatbonton's facts are right; there is every reason for optimism. The country cannot go down the drain. What the college of Catholic Bishops claims cannot be anything but true: the rich are becoming richer, and the poor worse off these days than ever before. But, by gad, the population does not only grow by increases by leaps and bounds. With that as the given, the country can not but settle for anything other than Renewal. What else, pray, is there to do? Filipinos have discovered a new space after all. With his labor scattered the world over, a diasporic dispersal is configured, as it were, beyond the very spread of the archipelago over a small kerchief of water off the coast of continental Asia. A force seven million strong is providing at least a tenth of the money for the national budget although Inday has perforce to make some of that money by scouring pots and pans in Spain and Italy and singing Singaporean babies to sleep.

It only stands to reason that the Filipino must cherish what has always been his, the seven thousand one-hundred-and-seven islands that are in fact his home. Ecotourism is consciously becoming functional as an idea. The particulars of self-preservation have entered public policy. That more of this inspiration gets embedded in the national stream of thought is probably a wish that many would even want to transform into prayer. Particularly in the delicate cuddly tarsiers of Bohol, more symbolic than the mere zoological rarity that Prince Charles took them to be, is our ecotourism's and the country's very future. Once the tarsiers go, so will Bohol and the rest of us, underground rivers and enchanted coral gardens and all.

Along with nearly a hundred years of English and the culture of the West, which English has been bringing over and has been responsible for, the Filipino has drawn from the West a culture that has inculcated in him a sense of determinacy. This is a feel for closure that makes us share in nearly all the anxiety of the West rather than turn away. It may not be right but it probably is the price to pay for having been "discovered" by Magellan and managed to take up other roles besides. In the books that Cristina Pantoja Hidalgo describes in her essay are the lived lives of the last seventy or eighty years, evocations and images of the national experience available in the rich and often colorful proportions that Filipino imagination has wrought. As a body of work, this was never intended to prove anything beyond proof of a potential for expressions of creativity and talent. Somewhere along the way, together with the will toward self-definition, the Filipino is discovering that he is worthy of the practice of the novelist's art. Incidentally, he also knows by now that perhaps in this practice lies an advocacy.

Perhaps the literature can be faulted for being more provincial and national, or maybe even more painfully nationalistic than it should be. The Katipunan has not quite done with him. In any event, the provincial bias cannot but eventually wear out. No one, to our knowledge, would want to return to romance, be it imagined like Alexandre Dumas's or real like that of M. de la Geroniere's. Kitsch and its many varieties have taken over; in any event, a hundred years of diddling the second growth forests of colonialism has imbued Filipinos with the Heideggerian sense of being that history invariably finds human lives responding to.

Part one
Unusual Philippines

Translated from the French by Eileen Powis

A resort awaiting guests in Palawan.

What is ecotourism ?

Translated from the French by
Brigitte Liss and Pascaline Petit

In praising tourism as essential to the development of the human race obvious facts must be taken into consideration. As an activity generating employment and prompting investments, tourism constitutes a factor of economic growth which mobilizes a host of productive activities in the countries favouring its development by involving their natives in a substantial and diversified manner. It also contributes to extending cultural exchanges and peaceful relations between peoples, through direct contacts and mutual recognition.

Moreover, tourism has the unparalleled and sustainable potential to participate in the progress of man owing to the permanency of infrastructures and the irreversible advancement of customs. Directly linked to the evolution of global economy and of disposable personal incomes, the tourism industry will continue to progress over the next decades.

Indeed, the World Tourism Organization has reported a turnover exceeding 450 billion US dollars in 1996 and has predicted an unflagging annual growth rate of more than 4 percent until the year 2010. However, these euphoric prospects should be qualified by hard facts. First, an ecological, social and cultural degradation has often proved to be the side effect of this industry. In order to perpetuate its activity, tourism should protect its raisons d'être : its environmental resources and its heritage. Travel consumers are finally becoming increasingly aware of the negative impact of tourism on the environment and are selecting destinations where such an effect is combatted.

Ecotourism intends to meet these concerns. In striving to combine the desire for a development in tourism and the conservation of various natural and cultural sites which are its "raw materials", it constitutes an alternative form of tourism that must become a primary goal as described by the World Wide Fund (WWF) : "Tourism to protected areas of outstanding natural beauty, extraordinary ecological interest, and pristine wilderness has been greatly increasing over the past two decades. Tourism in protected areas, also referred to as nature tourism or ecotourism, has rapidly evolved from a pastime of a select few, to a range of activities that encompasses a lot of people pursuing a wide variety of interests in nature."

In 1996, his Royal Majesty the Prince of Wales summed up this new opportunity offered to world tourism : "For many places, the process of uglification through insensitive development for mass tourism and the destruction of natural

environments, townscapes and fragile ecosystems have demonstrated, vividly and tragically, the limits to sustainability. It is encouraging, however, to discover that there are a handful of sensitive developers, planners, architects and builders who recognize that an alternative and sustainable path to tourism development is the only guarantee for long-term profitability and of preserving the irreplaceable beauty of our environment for our descendants." In this context, ecotourism swiftly proved to be the very basis of tourism in South East Asia and particularly in the Philippines.

In choosing "Ecotourism, Growing with Nature" as the theme for Manila's candidacy for the 2002 World Exposition, the Philippine Government has given top priority to this sector based on President Fidel V. Ramos' conviction: "Travel and tourism will lead the Asian economies in the twenty first century."

Considering the remarkable natural resources and the topography of the archipelago as well as the hospitality and open-mindedness of the Filipinos, this theme was in fact a given. It emphasizes an interactive approach to Nature in order to prevent it from deteriorating and to preserve the innumerable benefits it has to offer.

Ecotourism fits in with the spirit of the United Nations' Conference on the Environment and Development, which took place in Rio de Janeiro in 1992, and reflects the policy implemented by the Department of Tourism of the Philippines. The various initiatives, taken over by regional and local organizations, either private or public, have begun to concretize the principles of ecotourism concerning the protection of increasingly visited sites and the creation of new ways of discovering the most attractive, but often the most vulnerable areas, in the Philippines.

A close watch is increasingly kept over the fauna, the forests, the beaches and the sea bottom. Pillagers, polluters and poachers of all sorts are systematically dissuaded by the strict enforcement of the law. Nevertheless, informing and educating the natives and the travellers on the vulnerability of ecosystems is a far more efficient method of obtaining respect and protection for these endangered areas. The backbone of the development and expansion of ecotourism in the country is its acceptance by Filipinos for whom it is becoming a state of mind. Under these conditions, the expansion of tourism in the archipelago will grow consistently and harmoniously on a long-term basis.

Furthermore, travellers from the world over will, for a long time and in a privileged manner, be able to associate the archipelago with leisure and the spirit of adventure.

Between 1996 and 1997, the contribution of tourism to the gross national product has more than doubled. Everything prompts us to believe that this is just the beginning.

Threatened by extinction, the tarsier, the world's smallest monkey, is protected by the Tarsier Sanctuary Center in Bohol.

Data courtesy of the Secretary of Tourism of the Republic of the Philippines.

T'bolis, the lotus people

Photo facing the title page
The lake dwelling of the T'bolis.

Above
Navigation across the lotus fields.

Along the banks of Lake Sebu, on the island of Mindanao, a people is still resisting the invasive pressure of the modern world, having come close enough to not want any part of it. The T'bolis are fighting the last battle. An unequal struggle to continue to weave marvelous fabrics, fish tilapia, remain as sensitive to the laws of a sometimes intolerant nature like the fragile lotus flower. It opens at dawn, carpeting with pink the dark lake on which thousands of corollas float, only to close up again at the sun's first rays...

They are hunters, farmers, craftsmen and fishermen. Extremely gregarious, the T'bolis believe they are sheltered from the modern world, isolated behind the peaks and rocks of the Tiruay Mountains in the province of South Cotabato. In this region invaded by dense forests carved up by the many valleys, lakes lap the shores and rivers flow in peace and tranquility. And its inhabitants have long lived far from the turbulence of this century.

But for the last few decades, the modern world has come closer to the T'bolis. Hundreds of years ago, it had already knocked on their door. And the T'bolis must now confront the same challenge as other tribal peoples throughout the world: finding a balance between the riches of the ancient world and the promises of this new one that they reject.

Tilapia fishing using a dip net.

A giant tilapia fish pond.

Opposite page
The carabao is also
a means of transport.

Below
The costumed festival.

They are familiar with it without adopting the values foreign to them. That which is without value or use in our eyes and is thrown away, scattered or abandoned, they take and recycle into art objects. Copper faucets, doorknobs, old padlocks or empty cans are transformed by the village forges. All these objects adorn the women's arms in the form of magnificent jewelry, decorate the inside of their houses on piles having been turned into fine sculpture, or find a use as tools after their transformation.

Village dance.

In the rice paddy.

The T'bolis reject Occidental culture and its encroachment on the entire world that risks destroying their distinct characteristics. Certainly, like many others, they encourage beauty, but they do not recognize it as universal. For them, far from fashion magazines, beauty remains the same as it was for their ancestors, with elaborate and colorful costumes, traditionally made-up faces and expressions that have not changed for centuries. Fashion is not just a simple visual image. It is an aura that comes from within. It is rare that a T'boli woman goes out without finery and the T'bolis are excellent jewelers who make earrings, bracelets, finger and toe rings and magnificent necklaces. And these are the objects that help the beauty to reveal itself, to shine.

The T'bolis' dwellings recall the strength that the group finds in anchoring itself in its culture. The scanty houses on piles, made of bamboo and covered with a straw roof, seem to be from another era. The interior, often a single large room, welcomes a dozen people who only go out very rarely, sometimes just once a week. The houses are simple and austere in the image of this mountain people still searching for solutions in their past.

A rustic bamboo forge
for bronze jewelry and gold plate.

The T'bolis have always had a policy of exchange, refining over the centuries a culture fashioned to suit themselves, a culture made up of ancestral traditions and external contributions. They have observed the dictates of trade by negotiating consumer goods with the out-side world for a long time. Their Moslem neighbors were often their

Eating betel.

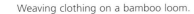

Weaving clothing on a bamboo loom.

intermediaries, in this way introducing new cultural contributions such as musical instruments and elements of traditional costume. Well before the arrival of the Spaniards in the 16th century, the Moslems and Chinese traded in this wild and almost inaccessible region. Objects can still be found from the Ming dynasty in the T'bolis' homes and culinary traditions often recall those of the Chinese. This ancestral tradition of opening up to the outside world has also taught the T'bolis to resist in order for their culture to survive. This determination to be independent, which has accepted new influences and new ideas, has also ensured them the acknowledgement of their difference and, especially, their freedom.

Gathering lotus.

Hunting for aquatic snails
under the lotus leaves.

This was the case for centuries on end, but now the environment is no longer the same. Many immigrants from the lowlands have ventured onto the high plateaus of the T'bolis in search of resources and wealth. If flight was possible in the past when invaders threatened the equilibrium of the ethnic group, the lands are now no longer unsullied by human presence. Nowhere is there a place where modern man has not imposed his way of living and such is not the way of the T'bolis.

Preparing food.

The T'bolis have never liked war - their tactic has always been to flee. But now, they must fight so that their culture can survive. A Catholic mission, present for the last thirty years, is helping them in their battle. The priests have adapted the mass to the cultural sensitivities of the ethnic group and a people has united behind the cross in a difficult struggle. The Catholic celebrations have integrated the local rituals and music, and here, religious images do not depict a beautiful blond angel with a chalk-white face brandishing its spear on a pale, sturdy steed.

And above all, the missionaries have helped translate the "Todbolul," the long and unique epic poem that the women sing. It can last for more than six hours and sometimes as long as sixteen hours.

Harvesting taro.

But the struggle must be total, so the priests have opened a school. They hope to prepare the young to fight with weapons adapted to an era that is not that of the T'bolis. Their hope is to see the young generation get involved in politics to better defend the interests of the population, especially in the allocation of lands and the control of natural resources. The biggest task, however, remains preparing the T'bolis to confront change. There are so many elements of value that must be preserved in their culture. Others must be slightly modified, for example, the dowry system. Before a young girl marries, the father must offer six or seven horses, land and many other items as well, to such an extent that it is then difficult to plan for the future.

The bath.

Setting off for the festival…

Planning is the T'bolis' greatest challenge today. The tribal political and religious leaders all know that change is inevitable, the question is how to go about it. Because for the last few years, life has not been easy for the T'bolis. Roads and electricity have made the region easily accessible and men from the lowlands have brought stereo systems, videocassette recorders and televisions, alcohol and weapons with them. They have also successfully appropriated lands from the T'bolis that their families have been cultivating for generations. The road toward modernism is, for the T'bolis, still long and full of pitfalls. And this time, they don't have the choice.

…the return home.

The living city of the dead

Opposite page
A replica of St. Peter's in Rome.

Above
A city environment.

Opposite page
1 The mausoleum-palace of a rich Chinese...
2 ...inside the palace.

The most lively and extravagant cemetery imaginable is found in Manila. A city within a city, a monstrous gilded sanctuary in the capital of the Philippines: a living city of the dead. Here, the sons of Heaven own country houses disguised as mausoleums. Their descendants come to revel around the tomb of a grandfather, an ex-noodle, cigarette or concrete king: a way for the living to share with the dead the luxury bequeathed to them.

The accompanying photographs are the first officially permitted to be taken of this incredible Chinese cemetery that extends over forty hectares. Before entering this other world, official authorization from the city authorities, the only ones entitled to grant it, as well as the consent of the families, must be obtained.

1

2

城佳注翼公楊

An urban ambience on a street in the Chinese cemetery.

The 40 000 inhabitants so fêted were all of Chinese origin. They had made fortunes in real estate, for example, or insurance. Grateful for the generally considerable legacies, their descendants honor, as is proper, their mausoleum. Moreover, the living make sure that the fortunes spent for the offerings favor their own professional and private success.

Guards survey the entrance from high walls that protect the cemetery. Once this obstacle is cleared, you discover an immense residential quarter planted with fresh gardens, with wide avenues that run alongside the marble dwellings, a striking contrast to the poverty of the surrounding areas. Each of the mausoleums is guarded as well, by aggressive watchmen, but once the visitor has gone past the bronze door a wave of blasting contemporary music hits him and he notices, around the tomb, the grandchildren of an ex-nabob in the middle of a spree. Whiskies, food, dancing… The dead too have the right to enjoy themselves.

Above his own tomb, the master of the premises doesn't blink an eye : he is Fernando Amorsolo, the Filipino "Michelangelo", who painted the

The entire family, including the driver, visits the grandfather's grave.

Opposite page
Here lies a major Filipino film producer.

Organizing surprise parties inside a mausoleum.

Reviewing for an exam.

Opposite page
1 Security guards watch over the safety and the property of the dead.
2 Professional musicians enliven the cemetery.
3 A postman just like any other.
4 The mausoleum of the king of jeans, unquestionably the most spectacular

framed and kindly portrait himself. All the other inhabitants of the cemetery have their own paintings too. Sometimes, when their wives rest beside them, they are portrayed in traditional costumes. Each vault has its own rosewood furniture, its Ming vases, without counting the hidden treasures. The patrols that survey the cemetery around the clock are not an extravagance : the dead are buried with their jewels and the women with pearls in their mouths.

About seven hundred employees maintain the premises. By car or bicycle, they drive up and down the flowered lanes. A host of shops sell soft drinks, candles and "kims," those fake banknotes that are burned on the altar so that the dead will have money in the next world. Thirty years ago, the cemetery was in the middle of the countryside, but an expanding Manila soon enclosed it. All of a sudden, the price for concessions went as high as those for houses in smart neighborhoods. If, at the end of twenty five years, the family can no longer pay, the mausoleums are torn down and the remains dug up and buried elsewhere to make room for rich newcomers.

1

2

3

4

Playing water games.

Today, next to dwellings constructed in keeping with tradition, are being built concrete ultramodern monuments in the style of summer palaces. Certain tombs, among the richest, are equipped with swimming pools tiled in Carrara marble in which the children joyously splash about: isn't that the best way to delight the defunct? "Mr. Marlboro," who made a fortune selling the cigarettes known throughout the world to the Filipinos, is one of the happy elect. But it is the mausoleum of the Wrangler jeans importer that remains one of the most astonishing. It is a genuine secondary residence: duplex, bar, bathroom, bedroom, television, video player, telephone and a cook in a white uniform to serve lacquered duck. That of the noodle king is regularly transformed into a dining area where foods responsible for the magnate's success is piled high. Once a year, the waiters from the defunct's restaurant chain jubilantly serve the family in a cacophony that resembles that of a waiting room in a train station. Elsewhere, children skateboard on tortoise shell-shaped tombs. And everywhere, the metal gates have letterboxes… for water, electricity and telephone bills!

Eternal and temporal repose.

Opposite page
1 The last dwellings of a business magnate.
2 Replica of an imperial tomb.
3 The children don't have any complexes about their ancestors.
4 A gastronomic feast in the mausoleum of the king of noodles.

Tuna fishing with bare hands

Photo facing the title page
The fish is immediately put on ice.

Above
A load joyfully carried.

On General Santos, in the southeastern part of the island of Mindanao, tuna fishing has created a genuine industry that stages a daily ballet with fifty boats. However, it is still practiced with bare hands, on board pump boats, those small crafts with outriggers the Philippines ploughing or Celebes seas chasing after the yellowfin. Our photographer accompanied the fishermen for twelve days on one of their astonishing expeditions and provided us with observations on the largest and unparalleled fresh tuna market in the world, a genuine gold mine for the Japanese sashimi processors.

The "Queen Lit's" does eight knots an hour, splitting, with its two lateral floats, the silvery mirror of a sea of oil revealed by the early morning light. After traveling four days from the General Santos beach, it should reach the fish-filled waters of the Celebes Sea in the afternoon. The dolphins once again slowly begin their joyous dance around the boat. For the last two days they have been tirelessly accompanying the calm crossing with child-like cries and clickings. From time to time, a shiny projectile skims over the deck with a fleeting rustle: flying fish rise from the waves and disappear into a tiny splash after graciously gliding one hundred meters altrough the air. The show, pleasant and entertaining is of no interest to the fishermen.

Their attitude is completely different when sharks are spotted. As soon as the first fin appears, excitement seizes the men, not because of the terror that these sinister creatures generally inspire, but because of the lure of profit. Sharks and tuna swim together and the presence of the former on the surface indicates that schools of the latter are about one hundred meters below. The bait caught during the last few days is then thrown into the sea. The sun-battered crew comes out of its stupor and each one nimbly takes his position. With a rapid and sure-handed gesture, the men attach bonitos and squid to round stones to weigh them down. In this part of the Sulawesi Sea, the nylon line does not remain motionless for long. More and more, the Filipinos from General Santos are fishing in this area rather than in Sarangani Bay, the other major meeting point for fishermen, only six hours from the

The fishermen take turns in the battle with the fish.

A weighted bonito used as bait.

The traces of the struggle.

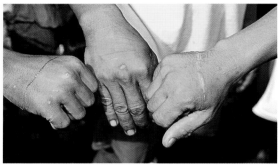

Filippine coast. This voyage is certainly longer and costlier, and the operation is illegal. However, instead of one fish a day, the fishermen catch one tuna an hour in the Celebes Sea.

Even if the tuna immediately bites the hook, the hardest is yet to come. The 1.8-millimeter line can bear a weight of 100 to 120 kilos. Holding it with both hands, the fishermen know how to estimate the size of their prey within the first few seconds of the struggle. "An 80-kilo fish has the same power as a jeepney (the famed collective taxi of the Philippines)," they note. Strength is not enough against such an adversary - the fisherman must also know how to use cunning. The fishermen's entire technique consists in taking advantage of the creature's distress as the fish fights furiously below them. The fisherman gains a few meters of line each time the tuna goes back up toward the surface and buttresses himself when the fish tries to go back down. After forty five minutes or sometimes an hour of struggle, the tuna is quickly thrown in the hold where cakes of ice keep it fresh until the boat returns to General Santos.

The tools: line and gaff.

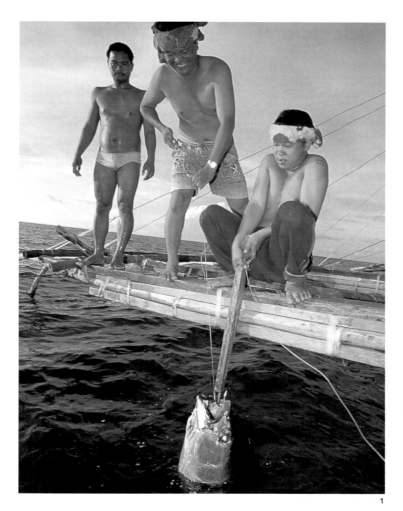

1

2

3

4

Bloody new furrows on the hands of the victorious fishermen have opened up scars left by previous expeditions. For some of them, their palms are nothing but bloody wounds. This is doubtless why the average age on the boats is between 17 and 18. Burned by the sun and worn out by fishing and the harsh conditions of life on the boats, the older ones are soon excluded from the crews recruited by the pump boats' captains. All of them long to bring in enough money to one day buy or be in charge of a boat. A captain earns on the average twenty thousand pesos (five hundred US dollars) per month, four times more than the crew members. Generally six in number, the crew's remuneration consists only of bonuses. If the catch is bad, the bonus will be less than five thousand pesos, about eighty US dollars.

The arrival at the fishing zones of the Celebes Sea or Sarangani Bay offers a picturesque spectacle. In general, about a dozen colored boats are floating near each other and their captains rush to ask the first arrivals about the catch. Of varying lengths, these traditional trimarans are as typical of the Philippines as the brightly colored jeepneys. The "Queen

1 Catching the fish with a gaff.
2 An 80-kilo fish is brought on board.
3 On board, the meal is of rice and fish.
4 Once the catch is placed on the pump boat's scales, the fishermen are euphoric.

Each morning on the "Gen San" beach hundreds of tuna leave the cold storage holds.

Lone fishermen can hand over their catch to the larger boats.

Lit's," the pride of Captain Rey, is among them. At forty seven meters long, it is one of the largest in General Santos, with a greater tuna storage capacity than its neighbors and, as a result, has certain advantages.

On the morning of the sixth day, an encounter with a tiny pump boat provides us with an example. Alone on his craft, an old man has just fished an 85-kilo tuna. He is delighted with his catch but it takes up the entire boat, forcing him to go back to General Santos before earlier than planned. After a few minutes, a deal is made : Captain Rey will take the tuna on board the "Queen Lit's" provided that he gets 25 percent of the sales price in exchange. Free to continue fishing, we watch the old loner, whom luck will smile up on tomorrow once again, slowly move off in the distance. Such is the harmonious life among the tuna fishermen.

Under difficult conditions of survival, solidarity and good cheer are more important than competition. Eight days are spent on board, eight days of alternating exertion and waiting in silence. The holds are filled with thirty fish and the "Queen Lit's" must now head home. The length of time the cakes of ice remain frozen always determines the duration of the expeditions : four days out and four days to get back to General Santos, where fifty-odd pump boats follow each other in an uninterrupted waltz of departures and arrivals. While some of the craft unload their cargo, others hurry to fill the holds with ice before undertaking a new voyage.

Upon arrival in the early morning, the frenetic activity on the beach of "Gen' San," as the Filipinos call it, is a striking contrast to the silent calm of the sea voyage. About an average of four hundred tuna arrive each morning. The number of fish caught determines the initial sales price, in the area of one hundred and thirty pesos (roughly three US dollars) the kilo this year. Until the price offered satisfies the captain the tuna will rest in the holds, sometimes for several days. Once the negotiations are over, the fishermen throw their merchandise into

Each dockhand carries a load of tuna.

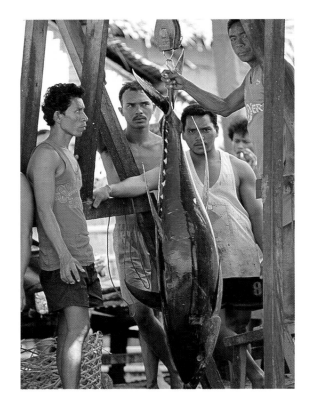

the water where a host of youngsters hurry to bring it to the stalls that stretch along the entire beach. The testers step in next. They are meticulous specialists who establish the definitive price of each boat's catch. Equipped with thin sticks, they test the tenderness of the fish by taking a sample that they spread on their palm to analyze the texture and color of the flesh.

In the midst of the buyers and sellers, a small man doesn't miss the slightest detail of the spectacle. Mr. Kawaï presides in a certain manner over the daily ceremony of the General Santos market - he is its biggest customer. Owner of the Pescarich company, this Japanese industrialist buys two hundred top grade tuna every morning to be used in sashimi. Kawaï just keeps these superb specimens' central section, the only part that has the exceptionally fine flesh required for making sashimi, those delicate portions of fish eaten with rice in the form of sushi.

Weighing the catch.

Quality control by the Chinese official.

None of the remaining 65 percent of the fish goes to waste, however. The Filipinos excel in the art of cleverly preparing scraps of tuna that are unappetizing for Western palettes. The ground fins furnish food used in raising freshwater fish. The inside of the gills goes into the preparation of bagoong, a very salty condiment that the inhabitants of Manila are extremely fond of. The intestines are transformed into grilled tripe. Grilled tuna eyes are one of the archipelago's specialties as well.

The yellowfin tunas are gutted before they are taken to the plant.

Kawaï's refrigerated trucks are waiting a few meters away, at the edge of the beach. The washed and chlorinated portions of tuna are taken to the Pescarich plant. Located on the coast, twenty kilometers from General Santos, this establishment, which is one of a kind in the Philippines, employs three hundred and fifty Filipino workers specially trained in Japan. The lightly smoked flesh, cut in to pieces, frozen at - 50° C and vacuum-packed, leaves a few hours later by boat for Japan (and, in lesser quantities and by air, for the United States). After an eight-day voyage, it is delivered directly to Japanese super-market shelves in the form of ready-to-eat sushi. The fortunate Mr. Kawaï has discovered a horn of plenty in General Santos. The extremely low cost of labor and raw materials as well as the recognized quality of the sashimi has brought Pescarich a spectacular and growing success. Orders continue to flow in from Japan and the United States and the plant is operating at full capacity.

All the transactions are made in cash on the "Gen' San" beach. Each morning Mr. Kawaï makes his appearance accompanied by a wad of bills. General Santos only has three hundred thousand inhabitants, far fewer than Davao, the capital of the island of Mindanao, where nearly two million Filipinos live. However, despite the enormous discrepancy in population, the two cities turn over the same amount of money, of which the fishermen earn only a very modest percentage. But in spite of their paltry income and mutilated

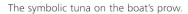

Leaving for the plant

The symbolic tuna on the boat's prow.

Mr. Kawai's market.

hands, not one of them would dream of complaining. Places are too rare on the pump boats, and the prestige of belonging to such glorious expeditions is well worth the difficulties the fishermen endure.

Seated in front of their boats, they patiently await a signal, ready to leap up and load the holds with cakes of ice and a few provisions: coffee, rice and spices to be cooked with the fish caught during the voyage will be enough to sustain them.

The boats are once again on the immense, silent expanse, leaving the noise and bustle of "Gen' San" behind. Only future catches and past struggles occupy their conversations and their spirits. Tonight, once again, cradled by the tepid wind and the murmuring of the waves, the vast silvery silhouette will loom in their dreams.

The terraced rice paddies of the Ifugaos

Photo facing the title page
The Banaue Valley.

Above
The water, the mountain and man's genius.

The city of Banaue is located in the northern part of Luzon, the main island in the Philippines archipelago. In the heart of the Cordillera Central, the two thousand-meter-high terraces are an eight-hour bus ride from Manila, more if the roads are flooded by the downpours of the rainy season.

They extend in a radius of 16 kilometers around Banaue, the most beautiful being found in Bangaan. Put end to end, these rice paddies would stretch out for six thousand kilometers.

The first image the traveler sees when he ventures into the mountainous massif covered with dense forest in the area of Batad is an amphitheater saturated with water. Nicknamed "the eighth wonder of the world", the rice paddies go up the slopes of the Cordillera Central. These terraces, however, are not the work of nature. For more than two thousand *l*years, by hand and using rudimentary tools, man has hollowed out the rock to survive: the Ifugaos were the ones who chiseled out the side of the mountain.

They still cultivate rice today, thanks to the skilled and laborious work of their ancestors. From digging to harvest, nothing has changed. Each Ifugao family exploits, depending on its wealth, one or more rice paddies which meet the needs of local consumption.

A product of man's genius these ancient terraces are, however, threatened because they do not lend themselves to modern, intensive, industrial rice cultivation.

The rural exodus and competition from the lowlands have turned them away from their purpose - providing food -, only leaving them the status of a cultural and touristic asset. But the maintenance of this man-made site and its ecological equilibrium seem difficult to separate from the use for which man created it. By cultivating the terraces, the peasants made sure that they would be perpetuated. From now on, constant vigilance will be required to maintain the terraces and defend them against destruction by natural forces and chemical pollution. One, UNESCO decided to classify the Banaue rice terraces as a heritage of mankind.

Ifugao hunters in early ceremonial costumes.

The village of Ban-Gaan.

An Ifugao hut on a rice paddy.

Farmers, the Ifugaos were also warriors and are to this day, hunters. One of their ancient customs has made them one of the most ill-famed ethnic groups in these mountains: head-hunting.

This practice, a relic of primitive war customs that persisted for a long time but was totally abandoned in the twentieth century, consisted in carrying out a sentence rendered after a tribal judgment. Not a trace of the morbid vestiges of these ancestral exactions exists today and only the memories of the rites and their representations live on.

All of the tribesmen took part in the "bangibang", the war dance. Equipped with shields, spears and axes, the warriors danced on the walls of the rice paddies, wearing the "katlagang" made of dried leaves on their heads. They then formed a circle around a chicken and slit its throat. The person closest to the bird as it neared the end of its agony was then supposed to finish it off. The head was brought back to the village, enclosed in a wicker basket and smoked. It was only taken out for certain ceremonies.

Rice harvest.

An Ifugao hut in the village, on the ground floor,
a living space, upstairs the bedroom.

Their reputation, just like the almost impassable mountain roads, permitted the Ifugaos to resist the Spanish missionaries. In the only country in Asia with a Christian majority (80 percent of Filipinos call themselves Catholics), the Ifugaos have managed to preserve their animist beliefs. "We, the Ifugaos, do not believe in Heaven or Hell. We believe in places of happiness or sadness," declares an elder.

When a member of the tribe therefore reaches an advanced age, the spirits of the deceased are invoked so that he reaches the kadhuhayan (house of the beautiful death). If this is not done, the defunct will end up in the kapitihand (house of the bad death).

The Ifugaos are a mystical people strongly attached to traditions. Their daily life is impregnated with shamanistic practices during which the spirits of their ancestors or the power of primitive deities (Kabounian, Kubuland, Loktad, Khuduk, divinities of the sky) are invoked. The Ifugaos take their rituals very seriously.

Their most important god is the rice god, Bulol. At harvest time, the strongest believers bathe its effigy (a blackened wooden sculpture) in the blood of animals which have been sacrificed.

For the Ifugaos, any event is an excuse for a ceremony. Marriage, birth, death, harvests, a fruitful hunt... even the arrival of foreign visitors offers an occasion for the village to organize a cañao, a ritual feast during which rice alcohol and blood flow freely. During these festivities, the men dance, eat, drink and carry on interminable discussions. The blood of animals - mainly chickens and wild pigs - is used to prepare the soup.

Tapuy, the liquor used for these celebrations, is also a local product, even if the Ifugaos remain silent about how the Chinese merchants manufacture it. The rice, harvested at the full moon, is partially boiled

Opposite page
An old woman with ritual tatoos.

1 Preparing the pig for the sacrifice.
2 Ritual dances.
3 The sacrificial gesture.
4 Three pigs are sacrificed.
5 Age and contemplation.

The village of Batad, at the bottom of the cirque.

in clear water. It is then placed in an earthenware jar with a little sugar. The jar remains sealed for six months until the alcohol matures. Despite the attraction exerted by the Occidental world on the youngest Ifugaos, the ancient traditions still live on today: carabao (water buffalo) skulls still decorate the walls of the huts. The men wear traditional rattan jewelry or pendants symbolizing the god Bulol.

But the amazing demonstrations of war dances of initiation, real outlets for male exhibitionism, performed in traditional costumes - multicolored loinclothes woven from natural fibers - does not entirely mask a certain loss of culture.

The young Ifugaos increasingly hear another world spoken about and are giving in to urban temptations. The villages are gradually being emptied and are losing their dynamism. Nevertheless, those who leave in quest of another life often end up coming back to the sources of the Cordillera Central.

A child wearing the tribe's jewel.

Opposite page
A gallery of portraits of men and women
in ceremonial costumes and plumed headgear,
all made locally.

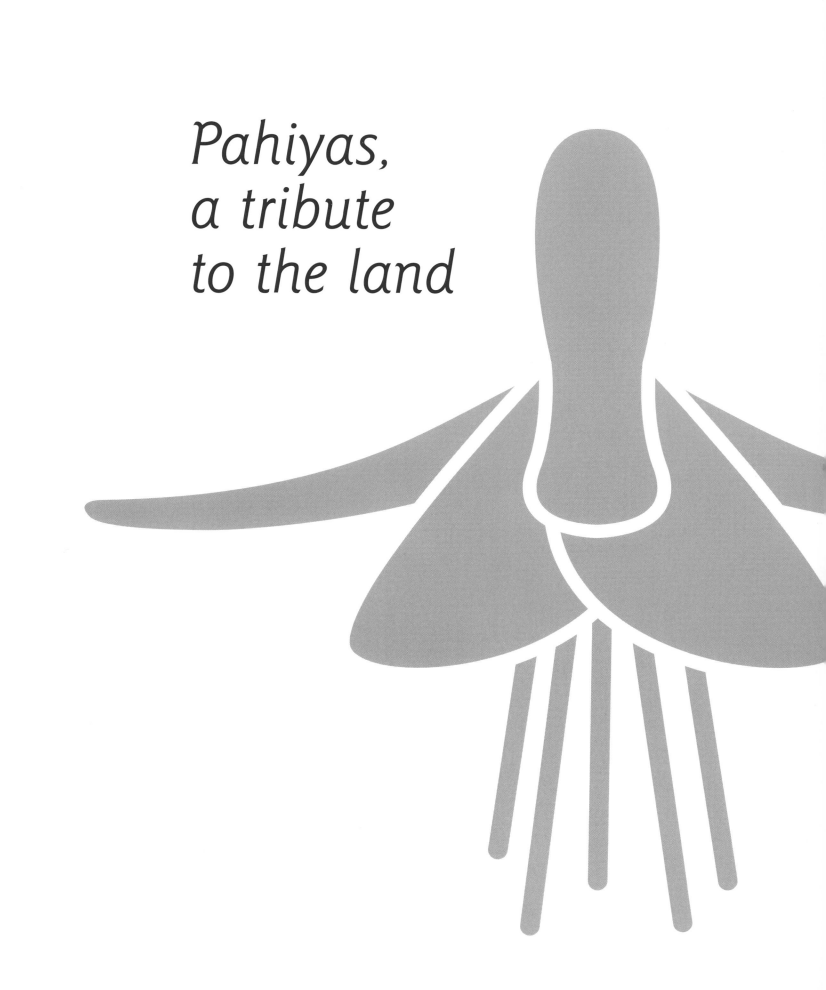

Pahiyas,
a tribute
to the land

Photo facing the title page
Kiping lanterns.

Above
Decoration of "kipings"
on the façades.

On May 15 each year, the town of Lucban, in the southern part of the island of Luzon, transforms itself into a gigantic plant museum to honor San Isidro, the farmer. The town fleetingly becomes a masterpiece. The fronts of the houses are bedecked with a mosaic of fruits, vegetables, sausages, leaves of rice paste and other agricultural produce symbolizing the resources of this highly imaginative rural community. The result is a dazzling blend of mysticism and pagan carnival.

When you wake up on the morning of festival day, the town of the night before is unrecognizable. The world that surrounds you is suddenly different, more colorful. In the space of a single night, the houses have been covered with a refined and varied ornamentation composed of plants. The festival of the Pahiyas has begun, a traditional local spectacle whose dazzling beauty holds its own against the Christmas festivities.

In the Philippines, the month of May is traditionally that of change. The first drops of rain arrive to slack the thirst of the parched countryside and herald harvest time. A collective feeling of relief greets a fertile year and the promise of renewed success for the coming season. If the yields are poor, only prayer can offer hope for better times. After long months of arduous labor, a visceral need to entertain themselves seizes the peasants and poor harvests can, at the worse, slow down but not extinguish this tremendous festive momentum. People spend money without counting and anguish concerning the future is momentarily forgotten. It is in Lucban more than anywhere else that this period of change and festivity is celebrated with the most fervor. Located in the province of Quezon, approximately one hundred and fifty kilometers southwest of Manila, the narrow streets of this small town wind around the slope of a hill covered with electric green rice paddies. Between the cultivated land and the volcanic mountains stretches a dense forest, more

Preparations for decorating a house.

Façade of straw hats.

The altar of San Isidro, patron saint
of the Pahiyas.

Saint Felicia, wife of Isidro,
closes the procession.

often than not, lost in a light mist. Tucked into the foot of this imposing landscape, Lucban is home to forty thousand people who live in small concrete houses and large colonial residences. Most of the population own modest plots of land from which they derive a relatively comfortable income. This affluence, however limited it may be, inspires enormous gratefulness marked with religious fervor.

Since the dawn of time, given the rich land and the abundant rain, the villagers have been thanking the heavens for placing their houses on the slopes of an extinct volcano and making a landscape and the treasures of a tropical paradise spring from its fertile soil. The arrival of the Spaniards in the sixteenth century banished from the family altars the effigy of the god of the harvests, venerated and beseeched each day, and replaced it with the enthroned statue of San Isidro. Among the saints, Isidro the farmer symbolizes the rural way of life. During the twelfth century, he and his wife, Felicia, became celebrated for their saintliness to such an extent that they would be invoked as the patron saints of Madrid, even though their official canonization did not take place until the seventeenth century. Even today, this saint is the one responsible for an abundant yield. Each year, when the rice harvest begins, he becomes the hero of a long procession through the streets of the town, a link between men and the master of nature. A celebration that blends Christian rites and pagan exuberance pays homage to this tutelary divinity. At the foot of the beautiful eighteenth century baroque-style church, completely covered with moss, behind the statue of San Isidro perched on a pedestal of chased silver, the crowd stirs and the festival of the Pahiyas begins. Everything is ready for the great day. The town's inhabitants have been preparing the festivities for several weeks. Flowers and fruits were picked, palm strips woven and bamboo arches built to be used for supporting the rainbow-colored tapestries. A week before the festival, the priest had walked through the town to determine the path of the great procession. Only the houses located along the route chosen would be decorated. The itinerary changes every year so that each dwelling can have its day of glory. The exci-

Glued wood shavings.

The colorful grotesqueness of models,
part of the universal rite of votive celebrations.

1

2

3

tement invades the homes selected and friends, neighbors and distant family members are called on to carry out a work worthy of the honor paid them. The cost of decorating a house for the festival Pahiyas varies between four hundred and eight hundred US dollars. It goes without saying that the success of the festival depends to a great extent on the spirit of solidarity and community : the peasants obviously cannot handle such a large outlay without help.

Nothing is too beautiful to thank the land for its fertility. Everyone mobilizes himself, young and old alike, in a shared burst of fervor and enthusiasm to embellish the houses with ephemeral masterpieces, as their parents, grandparents and many other generations before them have already done. Some of them have spent hours in the forest cutting long stems of bamboo which, attached to the façade, would serve as supports for the ornaments. They have picked palm leaves to cover the roofs or tobacco to frame the windows with tangled green fringes.

Others have gone to the fields to pick fruit, vegetables and the first rice grains, the favorite gift of the gods of old. At the same time, at home, deft hands were making small objects in bamboo, canvas or papier-mâché and preparing kipings. Following an ancestral recipe, these thin flat cakes are made of flour, rice and water, tinted with natural colorings and spread out on leaves before steaming them until they separate from their vegetal mould.

Cooled and dried, they become the translucent leaves that each villager cuts out, weaves, knots or threads following his own imagination, to form chandeliers made of fans or giant flowers. These are tied to the bamboo supports along with sweets: banana leaves rolled around sticky rice, puffed rice cakes that the children catch and devour in passing. The festival of the Pahiyas offers the occasion to taste as well as exhibit the local specialties. Filipinos from every province as well as Australians, Americans and Japanese come to be carried away and dazzled by the colors and noise, to eat, drink, laugh and especially to admire a picturesque tradition that is unique in the world.

Opposite page
1 Flour and cakes,…
2 Fruits and vegetables,…
3 Meat and sausages…

Below
…The façades' decorative themes make use of all types of materials of plant origin : rice and sugar for kipings.

Children are the kings of the festival.

The dazzling image of flowers made from kiping remain in one's memory.

Dressed in their most beautiful and colorful attire, the villagers sketch out dance steps, encouraged by the drum rolls, while majorettes and clowns parade behind the statue of San Isidro. Cries of joy and music continue without a break throughout the afternoon. Finally, the noise gradually becomes muffled as darkness envelops the hill. When the day is over, after everyone has opened his home to others to share dishes prepared for the occasion, what remains of this dazzling festival of popular art is a fused community and the memory of the most beautiful declaration of love that one could make to the land.

Lucban will return the following morning to its peaceful rural rhythm. The farmers will go back to their fields to prepare the furrows for planting. The welcoming eye of San Isidro will see them joyous and satisfied by a prosperous harvest again. This prosperity can be subject to any number of hazardous events, but the tenacious capacity of the human spirit to play and laugh will transcend adversity. And next year, the beauty of the Pahiyas will flower once again.

Opposite page
The carabao, a vital figure in agriculture, is itself in costume and made-up.

Swallow's nest "fishermen"

The Palawan archipelago, in the west of the Philippines.

A hidden Eldorado, a vertical world in which the last swallow's nest "fishermen" gather the caviar of Asia. To obtain this glue used by the birds to solidify their nests, the Tagbanua - one of the ethnic groups living on the archipelago - confront, with bare hands and feet, without help or climbing equipment, the sharp spikes of a fortress that rises out of the emerald green sea. Considered in Hong Kong as an aphrodisiac and an elixir of youth, the product of their harvest is highly coveted. Let us observe one of these intrepid young men whose many scars bear witness to their expeditions.

Sheer walls, bristling with ridges.

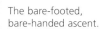

The bare-footed, bare-handed ascent.

1 One must sometimes dive
  to reach the deep hollows.
2 Each nest yields a few
  grams of white gold.
3 The torches are made from
  dried banana leaves and resin.

Exploring the caves.

A woven wicker basket slung over his shoulder, the adolescent holds onto the rock fragments with his fingers. Propping himself on the sharp spurs, his body undulates between sky and sea. He is fifteen years old and is undertaking his first ascent. According to a one thousand year-old tradition, he is pure, under the protection of the god Pangui. He thrusts his arms into a hole in the rock. Carefully, he pulls out a pile of dry white fibers in the shape of a moon: a sea swallow's nest, which he puts in his basket.

Made up of seaweed and saliva secreted by the swallows to cement their nests, this "white gold," from which an opaque cream is obtained, is used by the Chinese in soups that are reputed to have powerful erotic properties. The nests gathered by the Tagbanua are the best and most expensive in the world.

Traces of past harvests.

White gold bound for Hong-Kong

Erosion and winds have hollowed out cavities in these sheer cliffs, sculpting niches and creating distinct sharpened shapes that sometimes even resemble the swallows they shelter. The collectors carry resinous torches to light up these dark caves where the nests are found. A kilo of these swallow's nests costs in the area of three thousand three hundred US dollars, double the price of ordinary nests. This sum has no meaning for the Tagbanua: "We don't need money, any more than we need shoes or clothing. Above all, we want to continue to look for the nests like our fathers and grandfathers, to perpetuate the tradition." The collectors, and in fact all the Tagbanua, fiercely keep secret the location of this island with its sheer rock walls, which they reach in "bancas," outriggers. Only a few Hong Kong merchants prudently mention the existence of this site. From February to April, the harvest season, the Tagbanua "fishermen" explore the locations allocated to

Initiation.

their families and handed down from one generation to another. In May and June, the salanganis (sea swallows) lay their eggs. From this moment until November, the collectors spend the rainy season catching fish instead of swallow's nests. In December, they clean the holes and remove the branches and grasses to prepare for the birds arrival and the new nests.

The ritual takes place each year, as it has for centuries. Every day, at the end of the afternoon, the fishermen gather on the white sand beach. Using old pesos that date from the Spanish conquest as counterweights, they silently determine the value of the day's harvest on a fragile weighing machine made of cardboard and bamboo. The Chinese merchants then arrive from the neighboring island in their motorized "banca." Cases of beer and rum, bags of rice and packs of tobacco are spread out on the sand in exchange for the Tagbanua's treasure.

The ritual weighing and the sale.

Opposite page
Dividing the fruits of their labor.

The culture of red algae

Photo facing the title page
Kilometers of floats.

Above
Harvesters coming back from the sea.

Between the island of Palawan and that of Cebu, half a million Filipinos work in the Shemberg company's algae farms, factories and laboratories producing, converting and testing the precious substance carrageenan. Over and above its enormous financial success, the idea of the billionaire Benson Dakay, founder and owner of the Shemberg empire, has brought about social and ecological effects on a large scale. What links dog food and the transparent turquoise seas of the Philippines? The answer is carrageenan.

The use of carrageenan in the food, cosmetics and pharmaceutical industries are not well-known by the general public. The substance, however, is found everywhere. In beer, for example, carrageenan gives body to the liquid and clarifies it. It is also used to stabilize the foam on the surface. Injected into meat, it makes it tastier and juicier and prolongs its shelf life. It is mixed with pork offal and meat cut into small pieces to make sausages. An emulsifier in ice creams, a gelling agent in sauces and aspics, a preservative and solidifier in toothpastes and deodorants, it plays a fundamental role in these industries. Carrageenan comes exclusively from red algae, only two species of which, the cotonii and the spinosum, are cultivated in the Philippines. The cultivation of algae in this region had been a traditional activity for a long time, but it was not until 1955 that the manufacturing process for carrageenan was imported from France. The name of the substance comes from the island of Carragheen on the southern coast of Ireland where the properties of the eucheuma algae were discovered. It is mainly around the islands located between Palawan and Cebu, as well as in the Sulu archipelago, in the regions spared by the typhoons, that algae farms have been developed over the last twenty years. On Arena, Cavili, Tubataha, Bongao and Sitangkai, cotonii is harvested in deep waters, while the island of Sibutu lends itself better to the cultivation of spinosum.

Lines of polystyrene floats stretch as far as the eye can see on the turquoise waters of the Arena atoll. A few centimeters below the

Uses for the product.

A Shemberg floating
farm, part of the Dakay empire.

Garlands of young algae to be laid out.

Laying out young shoots.

surface undulate enormous bunches of cotonii ready to be harvested, whereas the young shoots have just been attached. The only access to the farms of Arena, twelve hours by boat from Puerto Princesa, the capital of the island of Palawan, is by air or private boat. Two hundred and thirty-five families have settled in this isolated atoll to devote themselves exclusively to farming. Each day, men, women and children go out to attach the young shoots of red algae to nylon lines floating around their houses built on stilts. Each family cultivates one and a half hectares and, on board bancas, surveys the growth of this precious breadwinner. Magnificent bunches that weigh two kilos after forty five days are harvested and placed on bamboo grids to dry in the sun. On Arena, 95 percent of the harvest is cotonii because the salinity of the water is not high enough to cultivate spinosum.

On Cavili, as on Arena, the floating line technique is used and the harvests take place every forty five days, as opposed to the bottom line technique that requires sixty days. On Calvili, the algae is dried on the

The harvest is brought in for drying.

Harvesting the red algae from the "bottom line",...

beach for three days. This method is not as fast because of the moisture retained by the sand, and not as clean as the bamboo grids of the stilt houses on Arena.

An international industrial firm is at the origin of this peaceful marine activity and its enormous hold extends over all the stages of cultivation, conversion and marketing. A giant in carrageenan, the Shemberg company began to set up and oversee the work of hundreds of families in the 1970s. Each family brought in a metric ton of dried algae a month that the company bought for about two US dollars a kilo. These purchases now amount to four thousand tons a month. From its headquarters in Carmen, on the island of Cebu, Shemberg manages a host of farms, several factories and a few state-of-the-art laboratories. Although the company has a dozen competitors in the Philippines, it remains the largest producer of carrageenan in Asia and the world leader in volume. In terms of sales it is ranked fourth worldwide with a total value in the area of sixty five million US dollars.

...from the "floating line".

Unloading onto drying grids at sea.

The algae is unloaded and spread out on land.

At the head of this gigantic empire reigns a Filipino of Chinese origin : Benson Dakay. Born into a family of extremely modest means in the Chinese province of Fukien, he created the name of the company by putting together the initials of the first names of his seven brothers and sisters and that of his own, a way of showing pride in his origins. The story of his rise is nothing short of miraculous.

Starting out with nothing, the eleven year-old Benson Dakay began to sell algae and, contrary to all expectations, orders flowed in. At the age of thirteen, he had managed to sell five tons of algae. At nineteen, he was a millionaire. He found his first importer-buyer, Michel Folcher, in 1968. Dakay acknowledges that this Frenchman from the Sanofi laboratory taught him everything. He helped him make his local operation the international industry it has become. While continuing to develop his business, the young entrepreneur studied science and commerce at the University of San Carlos in Cebu City. In 1970, he created his first algae farms and, in 1975, began to export carrageenan to Europe, where it has been used in large quantities as pet food. In fact, most of Shemberg's sales are still generated in this sector. But it was actually the creation of his first conversion plant in Cebu in 1978 that was the starting point for Benson Dakay's fabulous success. Fourteen thousand people work on converting red algae into carrageenan at this production site.

When the dried algae arrive at the factory, they are first sorted and cleaned. The first step consists in removing the nylon lines that remain as well as any parasites, then ridding the plants of salt and sand by washing them in large quantities of water.

Weighing of dried algae.

Hydroxide acid is next added and the mixture is heated to change the algae's genetic structure and stabilize the carrageenan. The substance then undergoes an initial evaporation process and alcohol or potassium chloride is added to solidify the carrageenan. After being put through a pressing machine, the dried product looks like cotton. At this stage, it is moulded and reduced to powder. The powder is made in various textures to suit the applications. Standardization is the final step in production: the different substances obtained are blended to unify the products. The last stage consists in packaging and labeling the carrageenan and preparing it for shipment.

Manual task of drying the algae on land.

Shemberg factory in Cebu, drying…

…and cleaning.

The last 10 years have witnessed the growth of the multinational's subsidiaries in Canada, the United States and Denmark. Shemberg Biotech Laboratory, in Carmen, was created during the same period. The laboratory carries out control testing on products treated with carrageenan. Another of the company's laboratories, in Pakna-An, Mandaue City, handles research and quality control. It tests toothpaste samples to verify their stability after twenty four hours, one week and one month. This "environment-friendly billionaire" has a broad, in fact, an extremely broad vision. It is said that he is part of that new race of Filipino entrepreneurs of Chinese origin who are leading their country toward globalization. Shemberg currently exports to thirty six countries and hopes to increase this number to a hundred within the next three years. Whether it can be attributed to his Chinese origins or not, Benson Dakay's business sense and strategic talent are incontestable. But far from the ruthless coldness that people expect from a business man of his caliber, they are astonished by this self-made man's simplicity and

❋

kindness, his refinement with its touch of humanism, his honesty and his Christian morality. A practicing Catholic, he often takes priests with him on his visits to the farmers. He considers it very important that the isolated life that he imposes on them does not deprive them of spiritual nourishment.

Control laboratory.

An imposing illustration of his financial success, the Shemberg CEO's pleasure yacht looks more like a luxury liner. Seventy meters long, equipped with four jet skis, two outboard motorboats and all the material needed for diving, this floating palace made in Japan only receives the visit of its august proprietor about ten days a year. Dakay's business does not leave him with more than three days free every four months for him to indulge in his favorite sport, deep-sea diving. The rest of the time, he rents his yacht to diving groups, usually Japanese.

Drying sites.

Packing the carrageenan.

Apart from the financial and economic developments, Shemberg's success has brought about important perspectives on the ecological level and exceptionally positive social consequences.

Carrageenan represents the product of the future for more than one reason. From the cultivation of algae through their conversion, the industry abides by a strict ecological plan that bans fertilizers, pesticides and all other polluting chemical products. It also encourages the Philippines to protect the marine environment. In fact, the cleanliness of the water is responsible for the quality of the algae and, consequently, the farmers' livelihood. They have, for example, stopped fishing with dynamite. Moreover, innumerable medical and scientific analyses have confirmed the complete absence of harmful substances likely to affect the organism in the short, medium and long-term. Shemberg has notably received the green light from the FDA (U.S. Food & Drug Administration), an unquestionably excellent reference from an establishment known throughout the world for the severity of its standards.

Uses for the product.

Not only does carrageenen make meat tastier and more tender, but this precious algae byproduct also presents the enormous advantage of lowering the price of meat and fish and thus making these foods available to the most disadvantaged populations. Injected at regular intervals into the meat by means of a press studded with needles, carrageenan increase its volume. The national veterinarian services have established standards for this increase that vary according to the geographical zone in question. For example, in the United States production can be optimized by a third, while in the poorest parts of Southeast Asia, producers are authorized to double or even triple the mass of the meat or fish being treated.

But that is not all. Shemberg supports more than a million people in the Philippines. In a country plagued with unemployment, this contribution is enormous. The industrialist, even if he has gotten immensely rich himself, has obtained more than decent incomes and a quality of life which any Filipino would dream of for sixty five thousand farming families. The wages, considerably higher than in Manila, allow the parents to send their children to school. And by continuing to create algae farms, Shemberg is making room for a whole generation that will be literate and qualified.

Ecological feats, economic success, a colossal fortune and social work: we cannot help but admire this entrepreneur's success. Carrageenan has stood the test of time throughout the world, and its European customers plan to broaden its application to other product ranges, doing more research and increasing the number of laboratory tests to determine as yet unexplored properties of the famous eucheuma algae.

Solidly established in the food industry, carrageenan is increasingly used in creams, nail polishes and makeup. With cosmetics, a gigantic market is emerging. Without any danger for the environment or health, the red algae with its extraordinary properties promises to hold a considerable place in the food, pharmaceutical and cosmetics industries of tomorrow.

Reliving the Passion

The Filipino Catholic community is the largest in Asia. It is among the most fervent in the world and demonstrations of an early Christian faith burst forth during Holy Week.

The stifling heat, the exacerbated pressure of the crowds overexcited by the pagan festival that accompanies the religious ceremonies, the proximity of an exuberant nature in the midst of which the ancient rites of animist liturgies have always been carried out, the ongoing temptation of the syncretism of cults, this entire environment favors the return of the Christian religion to medieval customs. Mystical or hysterical in nature depending on the eye of the beholder, these

Photo facing the title page
Flagellation.

Below
The Way of the Cross.

Buboy falls for the first time.

customs parallel traditions that have not yet disappeared in southern Europe. There, as here, the Church does not recognize these excessive practices whose sincerity and authenticity nonetheless cannot be questioned.

Man resembles the Son of God according to one of the Augustinian principles. Here it is taken in the strictest sense. The imitation of the Passion goes as far as physically substituting for Jesus in a realistic reconstitution of the event.

For the love of Christ, some believers have themselves crucified, their hands and feet pierced by nails, others flog their bodies with leather thongs or score their chests with ground glass.

We spent Good Friday in a Filipino village, Paompong, an hour from Manila. Abnormal excitement reigned that day in the streets, transformed into holy spaces.

An onlooker helps Buboy carry his cross.

The village had been busy for some time getting ready for the most important date for Christians around the world. It had decked itself out in colored decorations and set up tables ready for the cases of beer and soda to be served at the ambient temperature. The mood was that of a carnival. Men and women were wearing costumes from the year 33 A.D. as defined by Hollywood's ideas on antiquity: Roman helmets and tunics, veils for the Jewish women and leather sandals. The few tourists present innocently savored these preparations that served as an invitation to the festival.

1 A comb with ground glass teeth…
2 …to lacerate the back,
3 …on which scars are still visible a year later.

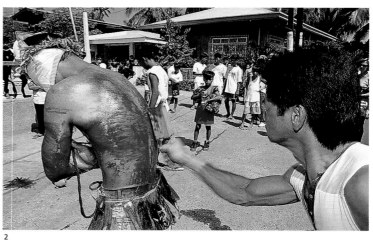

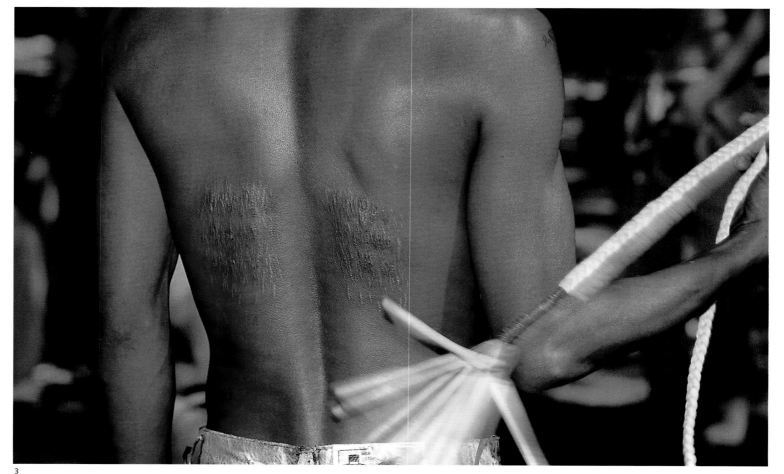

On the streets of Paompong, the procession of flagellants.

Certain spectators were preparing themselves for an ecstasy dictated by delirious religious devotion, others were little by little discovering the real object of the great reception : the many crucifixions. Men and women, in a reproduction of the Passion of Jesus, would be nailed onto their crosses by made-up centurions, their faces deformed by real suffering and the mystical and urgent expectation of grace. Hundreds of people were already assembled in the streets and on the squares. With the heat, the suffocating crowd of the faithful had already overcome some of the onlookers. The loudspeakers crackled out timid warnings by the police about pickpockets, the only group - and a not very wholesome one at that - that kept, when you really think about it, their feet on the ground…

Total exhaustion.

Buboy's crucifixion; nails are driven into his feet and hands.

Raising the cross.

A boy of seventeen, his upper lip fringed with a light moustache, harangued the public, which played its role, hostile or conquered, with a parable-filled speech. Buboy Dioniso still had traces of the marks left by the long aluminum nails hammered into his flesh the year before. He was being crucified once again, hoping in this way to cleanse himself from sin and save his elderly mother from a heart condition that doomed her.

It was noon. The sun struck down pitilessly. His long hair covered with a crown of thorns and dressed in a white robe, bare-footed, he carried his cross down the Via Dolorosa. An imitation Pontius Pilate, the Roman governor of Judea, approached to condemn Jesus-Buboy to death. The cavalrymen perspired under their papier-mâché helmets. Dozens of penitents flogged themselves with cat-o'-nine-tails studded with sharp metal, razor blades or ground glass that gashed, incised and tore the skin on their blood-soaked backs.

Three men hauled Buboy onto the gibbet, his feet placed flat on a block. Preachers passed through the crowd and distributed tracts as well as extreme unction. Centurions, with the malicious expressions of conquistadors, solemnly brought the nails. Eyes closed, sweat beading on his face, Buoboy repressed a long scream. With hammer blows, the "nailers," inured to such a task, drove the 15-centimeter-long aluminum shanks into his hands, then his feet, carefully avoiding the bones and tendons. The cross was raised on the Filipino Golgotha before the eyes of the entire crowd. Nearby, bare-chested, a few of the faithful flogged themselves until they fell unconscious, their arms crossed, swimming in their own blood. Some of them still found the strength to hold out the instrument of their agony and their deliverance to an anonymous hand, so that someone else could continue the torture by redoubling the blows.

Twenty minutes later, some of the faithful brought Buboy down from his crossed. They unnailed him and he collapsed, unconscious. Two women wept, their faces distorted by sorrow. One was Mary, the other Mary Magdalene. The apostles were there as well. The

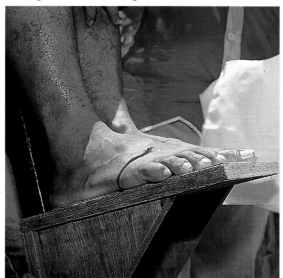

The stigmata of the morning's crucifixion.

The crucified is put on display.

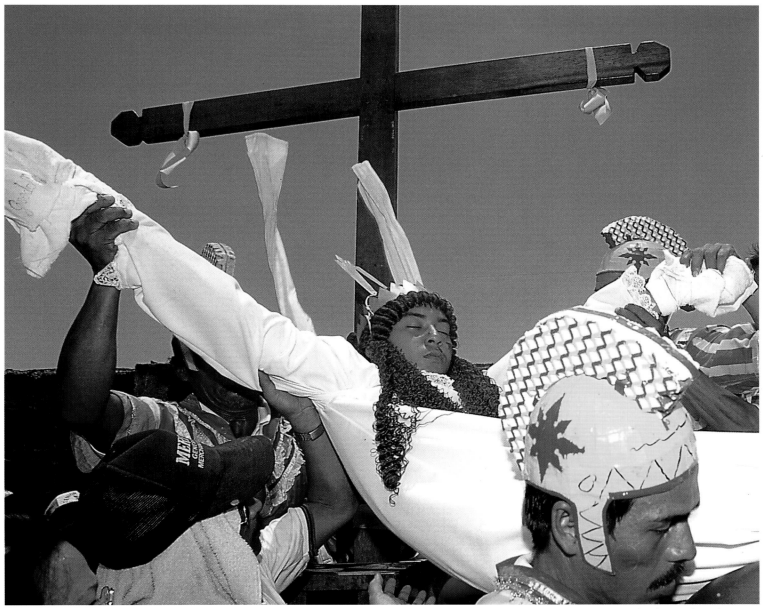

The descent from the cross.

Roman guards put on frightened expressions. One centurion cried out: "We are lost, we have killed the Son of God!..."

In all the provinces of the Philippines, men and women give themselves over to the same rituals celebrating the Passion of Christ. Most of them declare that they do not suffer: "Since I've been making this sacrifice for God, I have the powers of a healer," Buboy says. He hopes, like Lucie, who has been crucified for sixteen consecutive years, to one day hear that voice from Heaven that will order him to stop, conferring upon him at the same time the power to heal everyone. Other people who have undergone crucifixion disclose that they have no sins to expiate, no family to pray for, no illnesses to ward off, just the destitution and sorrow of a life they admit they can no longer bear.

Thanksgiving for having been chosen.

Opposite page
The crucified's mother, filled
with emotion, crosses herself.

Tau't batu,
the cave dwellers

On the island of Palawan, the life of the Tau't Batu tribe is happily spent far from civilization. Settled for centuries in the valley of Singnapan at the foot of Mount Mantalingagan (2,054 meters), the tribe numbers about two hundred people. Living in a state of almost total self-sufficiency in this 166-hectare plain owing to their agricultural yield, these men and women have built, over the years, a genuine microsociety governed by its own customs.

Living to the rhythm of the seasons, in harmony with nature, they nevertheless fear its excesses. They particularly dread thunderstorms. To protect themselves from this scourge, they migrate to the mountains at the beginning of the monsoon season, where they take shelter in caves for five months.

The forest environment.

During half of the year the Tau't Batu live in caves.

A period of intense climatic turbulence, the summer monsoon has devastating effects on this peaceful valley. Swept by cyclones and torrential rains from August to December, the Tau't Batu's small bamboo houses, although built on stilts, are totally useless in offering protection against the evil lightning. To escape from the ire of the terrifying Duldug, the god of thunder, and the downpours beat, down on their fields, the tribe leaves the village when the first showers arrive and disappear into the tropical forests covering, the mountains. Caves hollowed out over the centuries by infiltrations of water in the calcareous rock serve as their only refuge during the five months of rain.

Temporary habitat during the dry season.

Fishing with dip nets and bamboo grids.

Undertaken when the harvest period is over, this transhumance is a perilous expedition. The Tau't Batu must take very steep paths at the risk of injuring themselves on the pointed rocks. After storing the last rice harvests in their lofts, they abandon the village to its fate and climb the mountain loaded with the means of subsistence : provisions and utensils as well as their straw matting from the dry season in order to arrange their living quarters like those in the valley. The move is considerable and the ascent lasts two entire days! Once there, they must repair and strengthen the footbridges damaged by the typhoons, using branches and vines.

Extremely prudent, the members of the tribe are very wary of divulging the location of the caves and go as far as even denying the existence of these natural shelters. Passed down from mother to daughter, the secret of the caves is jealously guarded by the Tau't Batu to protect themselves from the outside world and to keep their last retreat intact.

Maneuvering in the heart of a genuine labyrinth of abysses and underground rivers, the Tau't Batu have adapted themselves without any difficulty to life in the caves, making all use of the resources found within. Employing hunting and gathering skills passed down to them by their ancestors, they devote themselves primarily to hunting during this period. Dressed in loincloths, the men skillfully maneuver the network of galleries several times a week and track game tucked away in the abysses. Lighting the way with bamboo torches, they use different hunting techniques. For example, trapped by a bamboo curtain built at the entrance to the caves, bats end up skewered on spiny perches set up by the hunters.

Children bringing back sugarcane they have picked.

Women making everyday objects and baskets.

Even more dangerous is swallow hunting which forces the Tau't Batu hunter to hoist himself up on a fragile scaffolding. At the top, he must patiently await the return of the bird whom he whips with a large racket made from branches.

Using all the resources that the forest puts at their disposal, the Tau't Batu also hunt with a blowgun, smearing their darts with a poison from the bark of trees, heating it until it changes into a reddish paste. This substance is also used for fishing, alternating with rattan bow nets designed to catch eels and catfish. While the men hunt, the women and children are busy gathering food along the way, picking up snails and land crabs, precious complements to their daily diet of tubers.

A time of respite and harmony, the five months spent in the caves are also the occasion for the Tau't Batu to indulge in their favorite

Opposite page
Local basketry

Poisoned arrows :
1 Gathering the rasped bark.
2 Extracting the juice from the bark.
3 Heating the extract to thicken it.
4 Smearing the tips of the darts.

5 Hunting scenes.

Woodcutting and preparation of burned land.

A woman playing the kuldong,
an instrument with three strings
made of steel fishing lines.

activities: playing music on a kind of three-string lute, making handicrafts and elaborating epic tales vaunting the feats of the mythical heroes of this people. When they return to their village in January, they must once again invest all their energy in the fields after having repaired the damage caused by the monsoon.

Agriculture, the tribe's main activity, keeps them busy during the seven months of the dry season. They grow rice, corn, sugarcane and other crops.

The Tau't Batu calculate their age according to the number of fields cultivated rather than in years. Upon their return from the mountain, everyone actively takes part in clearing the forest to prepare the land. Once this work is done, the parcel of land is set on fire to burn the stumps. A superstitious people, the Tau't Batu wait until the Pleiades appear in the sky to do their sowing. The harvests take place just before the monsoon.

The interior of a collective cave-dwelling.

The members of the tribe, grouped within several family communities, live in couples or with their entire family. Several generations coexist under the same roof. Each of these group habitats is called ka-asa-waha and everything is shared: work, food and tools. There is no hierarchy in this society. Everyone is considered equal and mutual respect seems to be the dominating quality. By way of a precaution, a wise man, the diklay, an arbiter of village life, equitably divides the resources and makes sure that each one takes part in the life of the village. Living according to the cycles rain of and agriculture, the Tau't Batu seem to living without any idea of time and, in all probability, without that of space as well, because the tribe is cut off from the outside world.

The diklay, wise man and arbiter,
is the senior member of the tribe.

Reaching them is a genuine expedition: the trip takes several days and the final stage is an eight-hour trek through the jungle. In any event, it is now forbidden to visit the valley of Singnapan without a special permit from the Manila authorities.

Part two

"Bayan Natin"
Our Country

In the light of history

by Silvino V. Epistola

V. EPISTOLA (B. A., University of the Philippines; M. A.,
Ph. D., Harvard University), and until 1991 professor of
Asian Studies at the Asian Center of the University of the
Philippines in Diliman, teaches philosophy and aesthetics.
Among his writings are The Home We Remember: Selected
Short Fiction of the Fifties and Pieces and the Old Inkstone:
Post-EDSA Essays; his latest is Hong Kong Junta. In 1996, he
was awarded the Gawad Pambansang Alagad ni
Balagtas "for literary excellence and lifetime achievement."

Photo facing the title page
The monkey-eating eagle, the Philippine
national bird, at Calauit Island.

Above
Prehispanic gold jewellery.

Trade pottery and some Imperial ware of rare quality dug up in Philippine archaeological sites show that Filipino-Chinese commerce began sometime between A.D. 907 when the T'ang dynasty was just coming to a close and the first decades of the Sung dynasty which was founded in 960. According to Ma Tuan-lin, who went around the quay at Canton interviewing merchants just returned from their mercantile voyages to all sorts of strange places beyond the seas, people from Ma-I, which has since been identified as Mindoro in the Philippines, arrived in Canton with goods for sale. The inventory included mats of very fine weave, pearls, corals of splendid quality, and seashells.

The World: Two Goals

Archaeologists now find themselves hard put to explain the fine T'ang porcelain which have turned up in many places in the Philippines. Historical data put Filipino-Chinese commerce well within much later Sung times. One explanation is that the fine T'ang pottery were not part of the regular trade but chance exchanges for food and other supplies needed on board passing merchant ships. Another explanation is that the T'ang pieces were brought over by Arab traders and bartered for such pro-

ducts of the country as betel nuts, ginger, yellow wax, sea shells and the like. What lends credence to both explanations is the fact that no distinctively T'ang sites have been found anywhere in the Philippines.

Of course, the Chinese did not just sit comfortably in Canton and wait for the world to come to them. They went out and brought to the world goods of Chinese manufacture and returned with what the world had to offer. The Chinese maritime merchants sailed out of their harbours on sturdy sailboats Chinese shipwrights had built for them to sail the rough and boisterous South China Sea. These ships were huge, one awed observer noted, like houses. The Arabs had likewise launched their ocean-going freighters from their end of the known world in West Asia. Like their Chinese counterparts, Arab seamen had mastered monsoon sailing, and this skill enabled them to navigate the long stretches of ocean from Basra at the head of the Persian Gulf to Canton almost halfway around the world in southern China.

To provide the staple of this international maritime trade, Chinese manufacturers developed the technology of mass production. Kilns scattered around the commercial seaports regularly churned out the huge quantities of trade pottery to meet the global needs of mass consumption as well as the limited quantities of what was known as Imperial Ware to satisfy affluent demand. For all that, no merchant needed to risk hard earned profits to shipwreck in unfamiliar waters or to piracy on the high seas. A way had been found to carry certificates in lieu of money or precious metals. These were issued for cast at, say, Canton, redeemable for the same amount of money on the other end of the long trade route at Baghdad.

SAILING SOUTH

Chinese commerce with the Philippines and the rest of Southeast Asia was supervised by the Superintendent of Merchant Shipping at Ch'uan-chou. The merchantmen going to the Philippines sailed out of Ch'uan-chou with the Northeast monsoon towards the end of the year, heading for the Babuyan Islands north of Luzon by way of the Pescadores. They followed the Western coast of Luzon southwards to Mindoro, a regular merchandising stop. The Chinese brought porcelain, gold, iron, censers, lead-coloured beads, iron needles and such. Filipinos came on board the ships, took what was offered and sailed off in their small sailing craft to peddle the Chinese merchandise elsewhere. They returned around April to settle their accounts with such products of the islands as yellow wax, cotton, pearls, tortoise shells, betel nuts, and hemp cloth.

Farther south, in the Calamian island group off northern Palawan, the ocean-going Chinese junks anchored in mid-stream and beat drums to announce their arrival. The people rowed up in their canoes laden with cotton, yellow wax, hemp cloth and mats which they offered for such Chinese goods as porcelain, coloured glass beads, lead sinkers for fishing nets, tin and such. The local chief intervened in disputes regarding exchange value, and when all disagreements had been ironed out the Chinese presented gifts to the people, consisting of silk umbrellas, porcelain ware, and rattan baskets.

Then the Chinese went ashore for more trading. After three or four days, they pulled up their anchors and sailed to some other island. Usually, they headed for one island not too far away and exposed their junk to the risky business of sailing dangerous waters with unmarked reefs, hidden boulders and shoals. What drew them to this island or that of a thousand perils? Only one thing. The highly prized coral trees which could only be obtained from the Filipinos living off northern Palawan.

Sulu was not at first a regular Chinese trading stop. The sea-faring merchants sailed past Sulu to the Moluccas, or as it was then known, the Spice Islands. However, thanks to enterprising sultans of Sulu, the islands grew to be a major trading port. They built warehouses where they could store the produce of the outlying islands, and they encouraged everyone to come and trade in Jolo. By the Yuan dynasty, Chinese merchants had begun to sail directly to Sulu, where they could obtain the much sought after Sulu pearls, beeswax, turtle shells, wood and the like. To the delight of the Filipinos, the Chinese had gold, silver, beads, earthenware, cloth, and iron bars.

Sulu pearls, though much smaller than Red Sea pearls, were very much in demand in Ch'uan-chou. Snatched from the depths by intrepid divers, they were always in everybody's shopping list. As you might have guessed, they figured prominently in the hair ornament of China's most fastidious ladies. But what really pushed the price for these rather small but almost perfectly shaped pearls was the affluent demand for them. Every scholarly official in the capital as well as in the provincial magistracies did not consider himself elegantly dressed unless he could button his robes from the chin to the floor with Sulu pearls.

That gold, silver and coloured beads figured prominently in all their want-lists spoke much about the Filipinos even in those far-off times. They were even then already a sophisticated people interested in enhancing their personal appearance. The word for jewellery in Tagalog is hiyas, a cognate of hias which means "well dressed" in Bahasa Indonesia and "beautification" in Bahasa Melayo, as attested by Jose Villa Panganiban.

ENTER MAGELLAN

By the time Magellan arrived in the Philippines, the use of jewellery had grown beyond personal enhancement to the realm of political distinction and official rank. Antonio Pigafetta, the sophisticated Venetian gentleman who served as scribe in Magellan's retinue, described the first datu the Europeans encountered in Samar, tattooed, rather old, wearing gold earrings. His company had gold armlets and carried weapons with gold ornaments.

In Eastern Mindanao, the Europeans met the ruler of the territory from Butuan to Davao. He was "a man grandly decked out and the finest looking man that we saw among those people." Pigafetta wrote: "His hair was exceedingly black and hung to his shoulders. He had a covering of silk on his head, and wore two large golden earrings fastened in his ears. He wore a cotton cloth all embroidered in silk which covered him from the waist to the knees. At his side hung a dagger, the half of which was somewhat long and all of gold, and its scabbard of carved wood. He had three spots of gold on every tooth, and his teeth appeared as if bound with the said precious metal."

Pigafetta had a really close look at the ruler of Cebu, Raha Humabon. He thought the man short and fat, and he was tattooed with only a loincloth and an embroidered turban-like scarf wound around his head. What really impressed the Europeans was "the necklace of great value hanging from his neck and two large gold earrings in his ears set around with precious gems." The Raha had his jeweller fashion two large gold earrings and smaller ones with gems, two armlets and two leglets as gifts to Magellan. That the Raha could give a visiting European such expensive gifts need not surprise anybody. The day Magellan sailed into Cebu, there was a large ocean-going junk in the harbour. Cebu was a regular Chinese port of call, and trade which even then generated wealth, was actively pursued by the Raha and his people. Hence, Cebu's wealth.

For One Who Had Once Upon a Time Wandered in Forests looking for berries to eat and hunting the wild beasts for food, the Filipino had indeed done himself proud. That was many thousands of years before. The food gatherers and the hunters had since disappeared from everybody's memory. However, their stone tools and their bead jewellery remained, scattered on the floors of his erstwhile cave dwellings and around the old burial caves. These now serve those who have to ask, "Where did we all begin? When?"

The Cave Dwellers

Archaeologists now think that Modern Man, Homo sapiens, the ancestor of the proud Raha Humabon and all those who have followed to this day, began arriving in boats six or five millenniums ago. They were superb seafarers who spoke a proto language present-day linguistic scholars have identified as Austronesian which they believe to be parental to all Philippine languages. The seafarers brought with them vastly improved stone tool-making technology which enabled them to manufacture superior implements for purposes undreamed of until then. But they arrived bringing something nobody had, an understanding of agriculture.

The earlier dwellers of caves in Palawan and elsewhere were Pleistocene people, children of the Ice Age. They had come walking over the land bridges which had sprung up when the sea was depleted because of the formation of glaciers and the polar ice caps around two to half a million years ago. Culturally, they were Paleolithic, Stone Age, people. They were designated Homo erectus, as they were capable of standing straight though they were rather short. The Tabon man, whose remains archaeologists have recovered from the caves bearing the same appellation, was given a different designation - Homo sapiens or Modern Man. When his fossilized skull was subjected to Carbon 14 dating, it was established that he had lived twenty four to twenty two millenniums ago. What makes the Tabon cave complex in southwestern Palawan so interesting is that in those far-off times, three distinctly different culture strains existed simultaneously in close proximity to each other. Guri cave was the seasonal abode of Stone Age hunters and food gatherers who set up their homes in the forests during the sunny months but quickly retreated to the caves when rain and wind came. They kept to the old technology of making stone tools, even if they noticed that their neighbours were using methods they had never before seen and that these people were turning out better implements. It has been established by Carbon fourteen studies that these Guri cave dwellers lived eight to four millenniums ago. Just 14 kilometers away from Guri was Duyong cave which was used as a burial site by yet another group. They had the distinction of using an even newer tool-making technology. They manufactured tools by grinding down the stone to the desired size and shape. For this, they earned the designation New Stone Age people. They were preceded, however, about seven thousand years ago by another group at Duyong cave. This was likewise a Neolithic or New Stone Age group whose members had the distinction of manufacturing really small tools and blades which they probably attached to pieces of wood to make combinational tools. Each of the three practised a different technology and lived a life-style of its own. Quite clearly, even in those distant times technological advancement did not proceed in an orderly, logical sequence.

The Jewelled Dead

In Duyong cave was likewise discovered an internment of such sweeping significance that Filipinos would do well to study. That it had occurred some five thousand years ago had not dimmed its importance, though it only came to light when archaeologists of the Philippine National Museum explored Duyong Cave and found just this one grave. It had belonged to a muscular man between twenty and thirty years old. On the evidence of two long bones, he must have been about six-foot tall. As his skull was badly crushed measurements could not be completed, and no real descriptions was possible. When found the body was flexed, arms and legs doubled. The funerary furniture arranged around the body established that this was a Neolithic Age internment.

What made this so extraordinary was the dead man's jewellery. Two shell discs with centre perforations were recovered. One was next to the right ear. Evidently, these were earrings or ear ornaments. A flat round shell with perforations along the edges was found at the dead man's chest. This just had to be a pendant. Quick to see the significance of the find, one scholar enthused, "This is the first documented jewel on the person of a Filipino !" Another mused with obvious pride, "Think about it, we've been jewelled for five thousand years !" Why should the young man not wear jewels! Look at the tools his family had chosen for him to bring to the spirit world. Are these the tools of one still mired in food gathering and hunting for meat? On his side he had his shell lime containers. Does this not show a determination to pursue the pleasure of chewing betel nut in the next life? In life, he had been healthy, said the archaeologists; muscular even. Certainly, the man knew how to take care of himself. Should such knowledge not include a desire to enhance his physical appearance? As he did not just pick up something the French call "objets trouvés". The ear ornaments were fashioned to look exactly like the way they did. They were made from the tops of Conus litteratus shells, and, when in place, they swerved to draw the beholder's eye from one ear to the other across the cheeks, thus increasing the visual impact of the face. The pendant hanging from the neck pulled the beholder's attention to the torso. Like the Tridacna tools around him, his shell jewels bound him to Micronesia where tools and ornaments were fashioned from shells.

The age of metals arrived in another cave in the Tabon complex, nestling about a hundred meters up a perpendicular cliff facing the South China Sea. Access was, of course, very difficult. The ancients used rattan to manhandle the large funeral jars up the cliff to the chamber of the cave now known as the Manunggul.

Today's archaeologists built a perpendicular ten-meter stair to facilitate the exploration of the cave. But the cave had a grandeur fit for the dead. For this, the ancients chose Manunggul as the burial site, and the National Museum elected to stay there with happy results. Of Manunggul's four chambers only two were actually used. The first one, referred to as Chamber A in Museum monographs, is seven meters wide and nine meters long. It has a rather large roundish opening that looks out over the South China Sea and some outlying islands. It is to this day a dry, well-lighted place. The second one, which is known to readers of Museum publications as Chamber B, is more like a tunnel than a burial chamber. It measures an average width of two and a half meters and a length of ten meters from opening to opening.

CAVES AND JARS

The field personnel of the National Museum remember with particular joy the sight that met their eyes the first time they entered Chamber A. Many large funeral jars with covers were all over the place. Skulls and parts of painted bones were strewn about the cave floor. The vessels they saw were either perfect, near perfect, or had only broken down where they had first been set down. And the jars were mostly decorated and painted. In

Coastal caves of Palawan.

115

Chamber B, the Museum field workers noted that the jars were broken, their contents scattered along the sloping floor. By looking at the shards, they surmised that the jars had never been decorated or painted.

At first, they thought that, of the two, Chamber B with its plain burial jars was the older one. However, Carbon 14 dating of the materials sent posthaste to the United States quickly corrected the visual impression. As the radio carbon showed, Chamber A dated earlier at 890-710 BC whereas Chamber B was dated 190 BC. The cultural analysis of the contents of the jars confirmed the radio carbon findings. Chamber A belonged to the Late Neolithic Age, and Chamber B to the Developed Metal Age. A diligent search of Chamber A failed to turn up even a single piece of iron artifact, but thirty pieces of iron were quickly counted in the burial jars in the other chamber. At last, the National Museum had archaeological evidence that the Filipinos entered the Iron Age in Palawan towards the end of the second century before the Christian era.

With the passing of the Late Neolithic Age, the manner of wearing jewels changed dramatically. The people of the Developed Metal Age favoured glass beads, thirteen of which were buried with the dead in Chamber B and none was found in Chamber A. Jade, which used to be so popular in the late Neolithic Age, had all but disappeared in the burial jars of the Developed Metal Age. On the other hand, carnelian which was unknown among the Late New Stone Age people became the jewel of choice in the burial jars in the Developed Metal Age. As a matter of fact, twenty carnelian beads were recovered from New Stone Age burial jars.

Interestingly enough, a metal other than iron was found in two caves in the Tabon complex. The first of these caves, the Guri, was occupied by people who came in two waves. The first to come established themselves at the entrance of Guri about 5,000 to 2,000 B.C. after the close of the Ice Age when the sea had already risen to just about the present level. Based on Carbon 14 dating of the artifacts recovered deep in the Guri cave, the people of the second wave arrived very much later, sometime between 500 to 300 B.C. The Early Metal Age was already well under way. It was at this time deep in the said cave that the other metal was recovered in the form of gold beads.

One of the two Guri gold beads was of the same type as that recovered from Tadyaw cave. Since gold does not decay, it cannot be subjected to Carbon 14 analysis. It may nevertheless be dated in association with other cultural artifacts which lend themselves to radio carbon dating. Thus, it can be said that the gold bead belongs to the Developed Metal Age about 100 B.C. to 300 A.D.

GOLD

Then, you might ask, as others have, "How did this gold bead reach the Tadyaw burial cave?" It is in fact not so easy to say, for very little is known about how these ancient Filipinos had lived. Archaeologists have entered their burial caves or dug up their graves and sifted through their funerary furniture and carried the artifacts to the National Museum. That says a lot about burial customs and about their ideas regarding the after-life, but it says nothing about life in the world. It is true that some midens have been located and dug up and subjected to Carbon 14 analysis, but not enough has been learned to reconstruct the life-style of these people. We still cannot explain how the dead man came by that gold ornament.

Is it possible that no one now remembers that these people of the Developed Metal Stage had come to Palawan on boats? That meant little until the rotting planks of fairly large boats were recovered in Surigao. Carbon 14 dating placed these maritime derelicts in the fourth century of our era. Only then did one begin to wonder if the ancients had not been the seafarers who scoured the island world of the Pacific for gold. And what did they do with it? If they had worked on the metal, what tools did they use? How come none had been found in any of the excavated burial caves?

Loud voices quickly assert that there had never been such tools. How could people who had never learned how to make a proper pot, fashion gold ornaments and jewels as beautiful and sophisticated as the jewellery European museums classify as "Egyptian" or "Persian"? If jewellery of such splendid quality had ever been found in Tabon and elsewhere in the Philippines, it can be said without fear of contradiction that such pieces could only have been imported from the great jewellery-making centres of world. If it can be proven that these had been locally manufactured, it can also be proven that such fine examples of the jeweller's art had been done by artisans who had been trained abroad or apprenticed to expatriate goldsmiths.

There were many places in the Philippines where gold was mined, such as the Cordillera ranges, Paracale in Camarines and Surigao. In the Visayas, gold was panned out of mountain streams. If the call of the raging sea was beyond resisting, they turned northwards on the South China Sea for the rich Chinese markets. With a sturdy boat, a good sail and inborn navigational skills, where could these people not go?

Gold in ancient Philippines all belonged to the red-yellow variety, with certain distinct variations. Silver and copper mixed in equal amounts made yellow gold, copper by itself produced pink gold, while silver alone produced greenish gold. The smelting procedures then in use could take out most metal impurities and all non-metallic substances from the ore. Gold was in those times classified into several grades. The very best in the trade had a weight of 16 or even 18 carats. This is the kind that was used in making ornaments and jewellery. Above this grade was the one known as "the lord of golds," which had been smelted and refined to 22 carats. The lowest grades of 6 to 8 carats were shaped into rings probably used for barter. They do not seem to have figured in the making of ornaments or jewels.

Raha Humabon

Did the ancients work the gold they had into jewellery or ornamental pieces? Pigafetta has more or less detailed descriptions of Filipino royalty wearing their jewellery, which obviously awed the young gentleman. He had also recorded that Raha Humabon ordered his personal goldsmith to make jewellery to be presented to Magellan on an important occasion, the baptism of the Raha and his wife. Outside of that, we know nothing about goldsmithing in the Philippines. Archaeological work has so far not turned up evidence of such an industry. No goldsmith's tools have been recovered. All we have are rings, pendants, earrings, armlets, leglets, anklets, and huge quantities of gold beads. Knowledgeable people have studied the finished products, and they have written long papers on the methods used. However, no one has found direct archaeological evidence of goldsmithing in the Philippines.

It is interesting to note, however, that jewellery made in the Etruscan manner had been recovered in a Palawan burial cave. This was a pendant bead fashioned from a gold sheet which had been pierced and cut and made to look like a series of spirals originating from a focal centre. This is the Etruscan-Roman bulla, the amulet probably copied or inspired by Egyptian (around 1900 B.C.) and Arab (around 1600 B.C.) amulets which

are still being made to this day. The spiral motif has been observed in a pair of dangling earrings recovered in Bolinao, Pangasinan. The similarities of design can be explained in terms of parallel development. For the Filipino artisan to pull this off, one condition and only one must be present: he must have reached the level of skill that his Etruscan counterpart had attained a millenium or so earlier.

The attainment of such a high degree of skill takes a lot of doing. The artisan cannot afford to be waylaid by such mundane activities as food gathering. He must pursue his art with single-minded devotion. This becomes easier if he enjoys the support similar to that which Raha Humabon had given his household jeweler.

Sad to say, Raha Humabon came towards the end of his era. Magellan had arrived to kill the dream.

Pearl oysters in Mindanao.

REFERENCES

- Beyer, H. Otley, "The Philippines before Magellan," READINGS IN PHILIPPINE PREHISTORY, Second Series, vol. I, edited by de Mauro Garcia, the Filipiniana Book Guild, Manila, 1979.

- Beyer, H. Otley and Jaime C. de Veyra, PHILIPPINE SAGA - A PICTORIAL HISTORY OF THE ARCHIPELAGO SINCE TIME BEGAN, Capitol Publishing, Manila, 1947.

- Casino, Eric S., ETHNOGRAPHIC ART OF THE PHILIPPINES: AN ANTHROPOLOGICAL APPROACH, Bookman Printing House, 1973.

- Combes, Francisco, "The Natives of the Southern Islands," 1667, in THE PHILIPPINE ISLANDS, 1493-1898, 55 vol, edited by de Emma H. Blair and James A. Robertson, Arthur H. Clark Co., Cleveland, Ohio, 1903-1909, vol. XV, pp. 99-182.

- Epistola, Silvino V., "The Day the Chinese Came to Trade," in FILIPINO HERITAGE, edited by de Alfredo R. Roces, 10 vol, Lahing Pilipino Publishing, Manila, 1977, vol. III, pp. 581-588.

- Epistola, Silvino V., "Asia's Ancient Common Market," in FILIPINO HERITAGE, edited by de Alfredo Roces, 10 vol., Lahing Pilipino Publishing, Manila, 1977, vol. III, pp. 617-623.

- Evangelista, Alfredo E., "H. Otley Beyer's Philippine Neolithic in the context of Postwar Discoveries in Local Anthropology," in STUDIES IN PHILIPPINE ANTHROPOLOGY: IN HONOR OF H. OTLEY BEYER, edited by de Mario D. Zamora, Alemar Phoenix Publishing House, Quexon City, 1967, pp. 63-87.

- Evangelista, Alfredo A., "Revolution in Tools," in FILIPINO HERITAGE, edited by de Alfredo R. Roces, 10 vol., Lahing Pilipino Publishing, Manila, 1977, Vol. I, pp. 156-161.

- Fox, Robert B., THE TABON CAVES: ARCHEOLOGICAL EXPLORATION AND EXCAVATIONS ON PALAWAN ISLAND, PHILIPPINES, National Museum of the Philippines, Manila, 1970.

- Fox, Robert B., "The Philippines during the First Millenium B.C.," in EARLEY SOUTHEAST ASIA: ESSAYS

IN ARCHEOLOGY, HISTORY AND HISTORICAL GEOGRAPHY, edited by de R. B. Smith and W. Watson, New York and Kuala Lumpur, Oxford University Press, 1979, pp. 227-241.

- Francisco, Juan R., "The Glint of Metal, How the Metal Age Dawned in Southeast Asia," in FILIPINO HERITAGE, edited by de Alfredo R. Roces, 10 vol, Lahing Pilipino Publishing, Manila, 1977, vol. II, pp. 393-400.

- Pigafetta, Antonio, "First Voyage around the World," 1525, in THE PHILIPPINE ISLANDS, 1493-1898, edited by de Emma H. Blair and James A. Robertson, 55 vols, Arthur H. Clark Co., Cleveland, Ohio, 1903-1909), vol. XXXIV, pp. 268-274.

- Peralta, Jesus T., "Pacific Island Galaxy," in FILIPINO HERITAGE, edited by de Alfredo R. Roces, 10 vol, Lahing Pilipino Publishing, Manille, vol. I, pp. 268-274.

- Villegas, Ramon, "Kayamanan," THE PHILIPPINE JEWELRY TRADITION, Central Bank of the Philippines, Manila, 1983.

The Filipino, his culture and society

by Prospero R. Covar

Translated from Tagalog by Romina L. Santos

PROSPERO R. COVAR has earned his Ph.D. in Anthropology from the University of Arizona. He is a professor at the University of the Philippines where he was Chairman of the Department of Anthropology from 1993 to 1995. He is the author of: "Values in our Quest for Freedom", published under the National Centennial Commission.

Photo facing the title page
Ati-Atihan Festival in Kalibo, Aklan.
Above
Street scene in Manila.

"Kung maliligo sa tubig ay dapat aagap nang hindi abutin nang tabsing sa dagat"- Balagtas
"When bathing in the sea, make haste, to avoid the rise of the tide."

Like the continents of Africa, Europe, Asia and Australia where the ancestors of man flourished, the Philippines is part of the "Old World." Homo sapiens came to the Cagayan Valley approximately two hundred and fifty thousand years ago based on the age of the beveled stones that the archaeologists found in the area.

In Palawan, human remains which came to be known as the Tabon Man, twenty one thousand +/- one hundred years old have been found. The existence of human beings on the island in the early years seems clear; small stones carved into utensils and dating back forty thousand years, have, in fact, been unearthed in Lemery, Batangas. Anthropologists claim these first humans were Australoids. Ten thousand years ago, a straight-haired race came upon the curly-haired people. The former cultivated land while the latter were hunters. Based on the estimate of Aram Yengoyan, it took three hundred years for the natives to cover the islands.

SI MALAKAS AT SI MAGANDA

Once upon a time, a bamboo was washed upon a shore, took root and grew. Birds came to perch upon its branches. One of these, a *tiktik*, heard voices from the inside of a node and pecked at it several times. To the bird's astonishment, the node split wide open. A man and a woman, one facing the other, stepped forward. The man was called *Malakas* or *the Strong One* while the woman was called *Maganda* or *the Beautiful One*. Malakas later urged Maganda: "*Alis na tayo rito*!" (Let us leave this place!). And, forthwith, the two abandoned the site for one of the islands where they had a comfortable and peaceful life with their children.

In *Malakas*, the folktale embodies elegance and refinement, in *Maganda* beauty. Small wonder the Filipino asks a never-ending string of questions particularly during childbirth: "*Lalake ba o babae?*" (Is it a boy or a girl?); "*Malakas ba o maganda?*" (Strong or beautiful?); "*Tuwid ba o kulot ang buhok?*"(Straight or curly-haired?); "*Maputi ba o maitim?*" (Faired or dark-skinned?). Here, an amusing trait of the Filipino race is at play.

The bamboo is depicted as a lifetime all-purpose plant. Indeed, it does serve many medical purposes; its trunks and edible bamboo shoots are cooked as vegetables; its mature bamboo poles are cut for posts, floors, walls, roofs for houses and for fences. Its small, thorny branches are crafted into fishing rods, blow pipes and musical instruments. The leaves are likewise useful for scrubbing surfaces clean and for making brooms. Other household items or even ornaments, may also be added to this list.

To strong winds the bamboo bends; it invariably yields; but after the storm passes, it returns to its upright position. Such is the resilient nature of the Filipino.

The pecking of the bird at the bamboo can be likened to the practice of the Filipinos in knocking at the door before entering a house and with the greeting, "*Tao po*" (Anybody home?), indicating that the one who is about to enter is himself a respectful man.

The bamboo, which bore Malakas and Maganda, is split clean in the middle and does not break into fragments. This is illustrative of the division of the Filipino ancestry along the maternal and paternal lives of the clan (see diagram 1 below).

The birth of a child brings happiness to both sides. As the child grows up, he is carefully taught how to get along with people, especially his relatives.

1 Structure of a Filipino family spanning three generations.

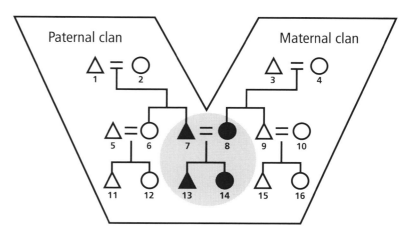

Relationships between family members
7-8 husband & wife • **7** father of 13 & 14 • **8** mother of 13 & 14
13-14 siblings • **13** son • **14** daughter • **7-6** brother & sister
7-5 brothers-in-law • **8-9** brother & sister • **8-10** sisters-in-law
7-10 magbilas (relationship between the husband and the wife's sister-in-law) **7** son of 1 & 2 • **8** daughter of 3 & 4 • **1/2-3/4** magbalae (relationship between the parents-in-law) • **7-3/4** son-in-law of 3/4
8-1/2 daughter-in-law of 1/2 • **11/12 - 13/14 - 15/16** cousins
1/2; 3/4 - 11 to 16 grandparents - grandchildren
7/8 - 11/12; 15/16 uncle/aunt - nephew /niece

Villagers taking time out from the Ati-Atihan festivities.

Malakas and *Maganda* were "united" in the bamboo. Hence, in life, they support each other in the fulfillment of their duties about the house as a couple and as parents. They are never in competition with each other, which is the appropriate attitude that parents should show to their children.

The Philippine ethnic language

The lineage of *Malakas* and *Maganda* is not confined to one clan. At present, the Philippines has more or less one hundred and twenty dialects, but these are all "rooted" from one mother language. Amazingly in fact, all of these dialects have the same names for the parts of the body, from head to toe, meaning that the words indeed sprang from the same root (see diagram 2).

The various dialects in the archipelago sound alike. They are comprised of vowels, consonants, punctuation marks and intonations. Through prolongation, accentuation, modulation and repetition of sounds, a distinctive pronunciation is achieved. The shortest word in all of the ethnic languages is composed of one syllable made up of a consonant and a vowel, (eg. *ka* - you); or consonant-vowel-consonant (eg. *may* - there is); or the new sequence of consonant-consonant-vowel-consonant (eg. *trak* - truck).

It is also possible to form a word by repeating the syllables (eg. *sit-sit* : to whistle) or by joining together two different syllables (eg. *ka-may* : hand). Likewise, repeating two words is also possible (eg. *gabi-gabi* : every night). Two different words can also be joined together to form another word with different meaning (eg. *hampas-lupa* : good for nothing/tramp). The forming of words are all the same in the Filipino language, i.e. by syllabification. The Filipinos use their language in describing their environment. The people, animals, plants, nature, events and other experiences were given names. The word denoting the name is called "*pangngalan*" or noun. All nouns have movements and actions - e.g. *tumutubo ang halaman* (the plant is growing); *tumatakbo ang hayop* (the animal is running); *humihihip ang hangin* (the wind is blowing). The words *tubo, takbo,* and *hihip* are root words called verbs, depending on their use.

As for nouns, the words *mataas, malinaw,* and *mabango* are adjectives used to describe *bundok, tubig* and *bulaklak* in the following examples : *mataas ang bundok* (the mountain is steep); *malinaw ang tubig* (the water is clear); *mabango ang bulaklak* (the flower is fragrant) Actions and movements of verbs are likewise modified - e.g. *ang pagtubo ng halaman ay maaaring uriing mabagal* (the growth of a plant could be described as slow), *ang takbo ng hayop ay mabilis* (the animal is fast), *and ang hihip ng hangin ay banayad* (the blowing of the wind is gentle). The words *mabagal, mabilis* and *banayad* are the adverbs modifying the action or verb.

2 Diagram.

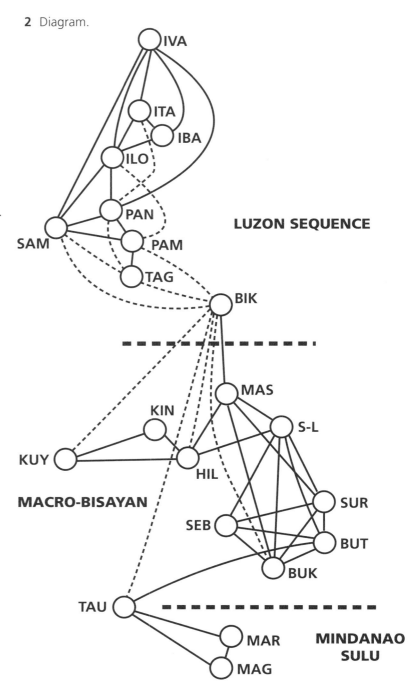

Classification and relationship
of the 21 languages in the Philippines
Source : Chretien, Douglas, Classification of twenty-one Philippine languages. (1962). THE PHILIPPINE JOURNAL OF SCIENCE

Legends :

Bikol	BIK	Maranaw	MAR
Bukidnon	BUK	Masbate	MAS
Butuanon	BUT	Pampangan	PAM
Niligaynon	NIL	Pangasinan	PAN
Ibanag	IBA	Samar-Leyte	S-L
Iloko	ILO	Sambal	SAM
Itawan	ITA	Sebu	SEB
Ivatan	IVA	Surigaonon	SUR
Kinaray-a	KIN	Tagalog	TAG
Kuyumon	KUY	Tausog	TAU
Magindanaw	MAG		

3 Bangang Manunggul, 890 B.C., Palawan.

example, is but a mere show, a means to attract attention. It is only superficial and one has to know her better to find what her real nature is. The following are examples of human traits linked to external physical features:
• The face is the mirror of the soul.
• A wide forehead is a sign of intelligence.
• High eyebrows mean aloofness.
• Eyebrows that meet in the middle mean short-temperedness.
• Cross-eyed means the person is good-for-nothing.
• Aquiline-nosed means the person is domineering.
• Plump cheeks are a sign of good health.
• Hollow cheeks are a sign of famine.
• Thin lips mean a person is talkative.
• A long chin means a man is a womanizer.
• A pot-belly means a person is corrupt.
The inner organs as well reveal the inner character of a person as shown by the examples below:
• *Mapurol ang utak* (rusty-brained) means stupid.
• *Pusong mamon* (softhearted) means a person is easily swayed by emotions.
• *Pusong-bato* (stone-hearted) means cold-hearted.
• *Salasalabid ang bituka* (to have interlocking intestines) means a murderer.
• *Maitim ang atay* (to have a dark liver) refers to a wicked person.

4 Internal/external features and depth of a Filipino's character.

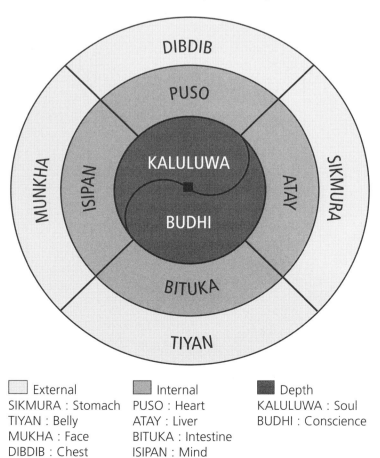

☐ External	▨ Internal	■ Depth
SIKMURA : Stomach	PUSO : Heart	KALULUWA : Soul
TIYAN : Belly	ATAY : Liver	BUDHI : Conscience
MUKHA : Face	BITUKA : Intestine	
DIBDIB : Chest	ISIPAN : Mind	

In describing the environment, occurrences, experiences, etc. the Filipino uses these four parts of speech. In nouns, verbs, adjectives and adverbs, the social culture of the country is manifested.

The dimensions of the Filipino's character

Archaeologists discovered in a cave, in the province of Palawan, a native earthen jar or *banga*. The find dates back to 890 B.C. Popularly known as *Bangang Manunggul*, the jar has a cover on top of which is a carving of a boat with two people on board. The one in front has his arms folded while the one at the back is paddling (see illustration 3). The boat seems to be headed towards the afterlife.

The earthen jar is of great importance to Filipinos. It can be used not only as a cooking vessel, but also as a funeral urn. Metaphorically speaking, the human body can be likened to it: both have an exterior and an interior as well as depth (see illustration 4).

The outer personality of a Filipino can thus be based on his physical body. Each body part is equated with a personality trait. As the saying goes, "*Sa unang pagkilala, ipakita and mabuting mukha,*" which literally means that one must show the good side (of his face) upon meeting someone for the first time. Maria's surliness, for

Religious icons are hung on tree branches during Christmas.

Still deeper, beneath the interior of man's body, lives the soul, which is set free only upon death. The acronym SLN (*Sumalangit Nawa*) which means "Rest in Peace", is carved on tombstones. For several tribes in the Philippines, the belief is prevalent that the souls of the dead remain in the sky watching over the community.

Filipino experience dictates that the soul makes the body move and a man's character is determined by the type of the soul he has. There is, for example, a *kaluluwang halang* (a soul that is not in the upright position), *kaluluwang maitim* (a dark soul), *kaluluwang ligaw* (a wayward soul) etc. *Budhi* or conscience, is the one that watches over the soul and straightens its waywardness. The check and balance between the conscience and the soul is similar to the balance between Yin and Yang in the Asian tradition.

Souls like that of Lumawig, who have attained a high status in earthly life, are regarded as higher than a hero. They are recognized as *ninuno* (clan ancestors) or *anito* (deities). They are respected; their birth and death anniversaries are observed, and the natives pray to them because they help the community in times of need, sickness, pestilence and battle.

The belief that deities nurture the soil, plants, animals and environment has remained to this day. It is said that deities can possess a man and use him as a stepping stone for their own ulterior motives. However, the deities, *diwata* (nymphs and ancestors) may be just vengeful. Thus, harm may come one's way if one fails to ask permission or begs to be excused for committing irreverent deeds.

THE FILIPINO FAITH

The belief and faith of the first Filipinos which revolved around the *kaluluwa* (soul), *anito* and *diwata* was called anitismo by Isabelo de los Reyes.

Even before Christianity arrived in the Philippines, several religious traditions had already reached the archipelago. In *anitismo*, the word *diwata* was very prevalent. The word comes from the Hindu "deva." Hinduism appears to have influenced the establishment of the kingdom of Sri Visaya/Majapahit.

When Chinese traders came to the archipelago, they brought along their religion with them. An example of Chinese influence is their cemeteries. The Filipino concept of *budhi* might even have come from "*bodhi*" of Buddhism.

Around 1200 A.D., Islam reached the Philippines and flourished for three hundred years. It spread from Mindanao in the South and all the way to the town of Sual, Pangasinan in Luzon. *Masgid* and *madrasak* structures are very prominent in the Muslim community. The former was watched over by an *imam* while the latter was directed by an *ustad*. The recognized leader of

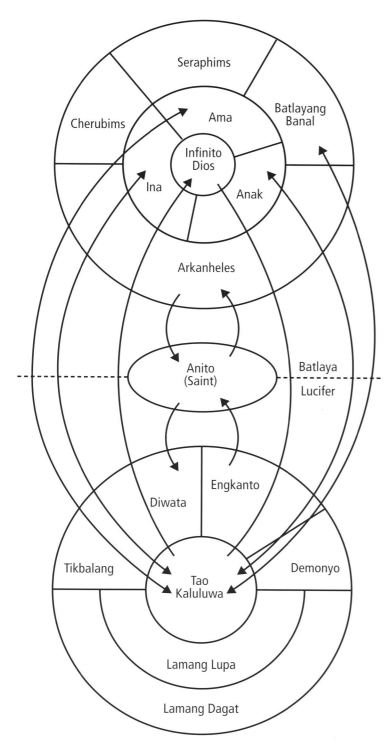

5 Outline of existing faiths in the Philippines.
(Covar and Reyes, 1997)

Infinito Dios : ....Infinite God
Ama : ....Father
Anak :.....................Child
Ina : ....Mother
Seraphims :..............Seraphims
Batlanyang Banal :....Holy God
Arkanheles :.............Archangels
Cherubims :.............Cherubims
Batlaya :..................God
Anito : ....Saint

Lucifer : ....Lucifer
Tao/Kaluluwa : ...Man/Soul
Tikbalang : ....Half-man &
                          Half-horse
Diwata :..............Fairy
Engkanto :..........Supernatural
                          being
Demonyo...........Demon
Lamang Lupa :....Gnome
Lamang Dagat :..Sea Creature

the community was the *panglima*. Having a status higher than the *panglima* was the *datu*. And among the *datus*, the sultan and his *rajah muda*, or successor, was chosen. Before the Spaniards came, sultanates covered the archipelago. They traded with China and adjacent regions as forces to the Malaccas.

In 1521, Ferdinand Magellan (a Portuguese who sailed under the Spanish flag) arrived in the isle of Humonhon in the Visayas region. After the mass at Limasawa, Magellan gave Humabon's wife a statue of the Sto. Niño (the Little Jesus). This statue was hidden inside a trunk for safekeeping. Forty-four years later, the Spaniards - this time led by Miguel Lopez de Legazpi - plundered Cebu and razed the whole town to the ground. Everything was destroyed except for the Sto. Niño; the image was found unscathed, inside a granary. The statue was thereafter enthroned in Cebu and came to be known as "Sto Niño de Cebu." This signaled the spread of the Roman Catholic Church in the Philippines. The proliferation of groups venerating the Sto. Niño has become part of Catholicism in the country.

The rule of the Spaniards and the Roman Catholic Church in the country lasted more or less four hundred years (1521-1598). On the eve of the twentieth century came the siege by the Americans. With them, Protestantism came as well. Like the religious orders of the Roman Catholic Church, the different denominations of American Protestantism divided the country for their missions. These were temporarily placed under one unit, the American Overseas Mission Board. Like the Roman Catholic Church, the Protestant Church began to experience fragmentation in itself. The converts broke away and established their own local, religious foundations. From the Mother Church, the Iglesia Filipina Independiente (Philippine Independent Church), the United Church of Christ in the Philippines the Iglesia ni Cristo (Church of Christ) and other groups came in this manner.

The different Christian Churches in the Philippines served as a model for the innumerable sects present in the country like the Rizalistas. This sect sprouted in 1930, thirty-four years after the martyrdom of Dr. Jose P. Rizal. Rizal is recognized as by other sects, such as the "*Iglesia Watawat ng Lahi,*" "*Tres Persona Solo Dios,*" "*Ciudad Mistica de Dios,*" "*Bathalismo,*" etc., as either God; the Son of God; the reincarnation of Jesus Christ; or a prophet. Among the sects is the belief that the soul of Rizal visits them through an investor or medium.

The use of a medium or channel, either a *catalonan* or *babaylan* in the vernacular, is deeply rooted in the history of Filipino culture. When the Protestants came in the 1900s, they brought along the Christian Science of chiropractice and mediumship; practices were chastised by medical doctors in the Philippines. Shortly thereafter, the spiritual tradition appeared in the archipelago. A center for treatment and worship was erected. Through massages, faith healing and barehanded "surgical" operations, Filipino faith healers became renowned the world over. Aside from the spiritualists, there was also a growth in the number of charismatic groups. The charismatic movement with the biggest following in the Philippines today is *El Shaddai* led by Brother Mike Velarde, a group slightly Pentecostal in nature. Prayers and healing are the main activities of the congregation. The illnesses that befall individuals are attributed to evil spirits let loose by Satan who cause havoc in man. *Siksik, liglig*

at umaapaw ang biyaya ni El Shaddai (solid, pulsating and overflowing is the grace of El Shaddai) is the catchy phrase of the sect.

Sects that criticize others for their beliefs and faith also exist in the Philippines. These are the fundamentalists who strongly wish to bring back into the fold those who have strayed from the path. They consider it their mission to spread Christianity in Asia, the Philippines being the leader when it comes to evangelism in Asia. The uniting force behind these fundamentalists is the "Jesus is Lord Movement" (refer to diagram 5 for the existing faiths in the Philippines).

6 Framework of the Philippine national culture (Covar, 1993).

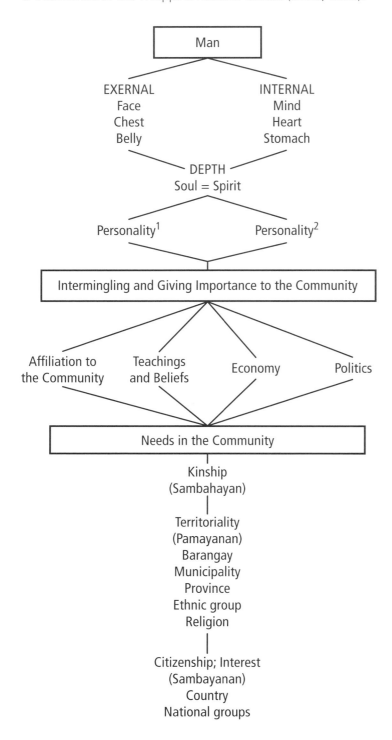

THE FILIPINO CULTURE AND SOCIETY

Let us take a close look at the interrelations between the Filipino, his culture and his society (see diagram 6.). As already explained, clues to the external/outer personality of man are found on the face, chest and abdomen whereas those for the inner personality are found in the mind, heart and stomach. Hence, the exterior and interior aspects of a man's body go hand in hand. However, the depth of the Filipino's character is seen through the soul. When discord exists between the soul and a person's current situation, he loses equilibrium. A man whose soul is not in the "upright" position or *halang ang kaluluwa* is said to have an evil nature.

The soul too has a color: an evil person is said to have a black soul while a person whose soul is white is pure and good at lending others a helping hand.

The Filipino is very sociable. He knows how to deal with people, to adjust, to mingle and unite with others in carrying out an action. Above all, he knows how to sympathize with another's sorrow as well as sacrifice his own life for his fellow man and his country. Filipinos, who work abroad as entertainers, domestic helpers, health care-givers, technicians and engineers, managers, experts and consultants are well accepted in most foreign countries because the Filipino knows how to carry himself and does not take himself so seriously.

The Filipino, as a citizen, abides by few principal duties to society. First, he defends his "Filipino-ness"; *Ako'y Pilipino, taas noo kahit kanino*, (I am a Filipino and I hold my head high before anybody) as the song goes. In his speeches, President Fidel V. Ramos often invokes, "*Pinoy, kaya natin ito*" (The Filipino can) with a "thumbs up" sign.

Another duty that a Filipino holds dear is a deep sense of gratitude or *utang na loob*. An example is the gratitude that children have towards their parents, which can never be fully repaid even when they grow up and start to have their own families.

Christ's death on the cross is accepted by Filipino Christians as a sacrifice for which he will always be indebted to God. Though man's redemption can only be attained through God's mercy and cannot be brought through good deeds, committing acts of goodness towards one's fellow is a form of showing one's *utang na loob* or gratitude to God.

The Filipino also responds to the needs of his society, particularly when it comes to making a living. In studying the history of the Filipinos' means of livelihood, its origin has to be traced back to the time of hunting, fishing and food gathering in the plains and mountains. Living in an archipelago teeming with natural resources, the Filipino treasured the land to meet his needs. Then, the time came when he began trading with foreigners. Nowadays, there is a continuous construction of factories in order to meet the demands of foreign trade. The skilled Filipino is likewise carefully studying the conditions and trends of global trade.

The political desires of the Filipino sprouted and bloomed within more or less ten thousand years when the Spaniards came, ethnic states were already widespread from Jolo in the south up to Sual, Pangasinan in the north. The revolts of the masses against the Spanish rule were related to their desire to establish their own states. The separation of the converted natives from Christianity in order to build their own foundations, movements and sects, was part of the national process of emancipation.

The Spaniards and the Americans recognized the different ethnic communities of the islands. The first provinces were even divided according to ethno-linguistic groupings. However, the natives were not given the right to choose their own leaders. The colonialists picked the officials who were to govern their community.

In the next generation of government, the Filipino became more concerned with food, age, gender and socio-economic matters. Local and national ethnic distinctions slowly begun to gain importance. Much national planning now revolves on the type and size of the population being cared for.

There are three elements essential to the growth of a nation found in the Philippine national society: *kamag-anakan* (family); *pamayanan* (community) and *pagka-mamamayan* (citizenship).

Two basic principles must be observed in nation building: (1) the organization of ethnic communities and (2) the division of the archipelago into barangays, towns, provinces, cities and regions, i.e. as territories of the citizen. The first is considered only when pertaining to an ethnic culture while the second is followed in running the political machinery of the country. However, there are initiatives towards self-autonomy in Southern Mindanao and Western Luzon.

Experts in the University of the Philippines believe that the different ethnic cultures in the archipelago

Walking on smouldering coals is a rite of initiation in Luzon.

are still intact, much preserved in the different languages spoken in the Philippine language. These have become useful tools.

The ethnic communities have a common form of expressing their culture such as through food, the manner and words used for counting, the parts of the body, the inner will, etc. For the Filipino, the body is used to perceive inward experiences while feelings are hidden ones laid out into the open. There is indeed a unifying culture to bind the archipelago. Moreover, there is a growing Philippine national culture brought about by the use of money, education, government, law and justice, trade, newspaper, cinema, radio, television, a national language, religion and others. In the end, a national discourse, which could be in the form of literature, is the one that would truly liberate the motherland.

Mabuhay ka, Pilipinas na bayan!
Long live the Philippines !

A nation renews itself
Politics and the economy in transition

by Juan T. Gatbonton

JUAN T. GATBONTON has worked extensively in the East Asian region as editor of The Asia Magazine (1965-69) and of Orientations (1969-76). He wrote a column on Philippine affairs for Asiaweek from 1975 to 1982. A collection of his magazine essays won the Manila Critics Circle Award in 1986; in 1993, a similar distinction went for Philippine Art, of which he was the editor.

Photo facing the title page
Banana harvest in Mindanao.

Above
Fisheries at Manila Bay.

The Philippines today is veritably a nation reborn. A long period of political and economic crises - coinciding with a series of natural calamities which included droughts and floods, a destructive earthquake, and the eruption of a great Luzon volcano - has tested to the limit the fortitude of its people. Over the last six years, the reformist Administration of President Fidel V. Ramos has put the house of the nation in order steadily opened the economy to foreign competition, and leveled the playing field of enterprise. In the process of rebuilding political stability and restoring the economy to the path of growth, it has arrested the decline of the national spirit and renewed Filipino optimism.

Never before has a Philippine government carried out such a coherent reform program to dismantle protectionist, monopolistic, and autarchic rules set over a period of forty years. Strategic industries such as telecommunications, transportation, banking, and insurance were opened to newcomers. Tariff walls were brought down, the peso was made freely convertible and restrictive laws were repealed to facilitate the entry of foreign investment and transnational industry. Public corporations were privatized - including the biggest steel mill and the water system for the whole of Metropolitan Manila - and export platforms were set up all over the archipelago to enable Filipino workpeople to combine with transnational capital and technology in producing consumer durables for world markets.

With local secessionists, military rebels, and Communist insurgents, an honorable peace was negotiated. A settlement with dissident young officers ended the series of coup attempts which had destabilized the administration of Ramos's predecessor, Mrs. Corazon C. Aquino. The truce that Ramos concluded with the Moro National Liberation Front in September 1996 cleared the way for establishing a pluralist national community.

The US Seventh Fleet's sailing away from Subic Bay on November 24, 1992, ended an era during which for four hundred and twenty one uninterrupted years there had not been a single day that foreign troops were not based on Philippine soil. Over almost a hundred years, the American presence had shielded the Philippine State not only from external threats but from disturbances to its internal status quo. Now that this shield has been taken away, the Ramos Administration has created for the Philippines a place and a role in East Asia. It oriented the country toward its neighbors and partners in the Association of Southeast Asian Nations (ASEAN) and made friendships with the East Asian countries the cornerstone of its foreign policy, while also broadening its diplomatic and trading contacts in the world.

In early 1998, the Philippines was in the middle of an election campaign to choose Ramos's successor. Meanwhile, a currency turmoil has broken out in East Asia - forcing a devaluation of the peso, slowing down economic growth and putting to doubt the future of the whole East Asian economic miracle. But it seems clear that, in the Philippines, the widening and deepening of reform will continue. Not merely has the new export-strategy proved successful. The country's external commitments - its subscription to the ASEAN Free Trade Area and to APEC, the Asia-Pacific Economic Cooperation grouping as well as its membership in the new World Trade Organization - are all pushing it toward an outside orientation.

THE CONTINUITY OF CULTURE

Like many other peoples, Filipinos pride themselves in a revolutionary tradition. In fact, the country's institutions and hierarchical arrangements have been very resilient and the political and economic culture has had a remarkable continuity. The Philippines is one of the few Southeast Asian areas colonized before they had developed a central state structure. Beyond the barangay - a settlement averaging thirty to one hundred households related by blood and owing loyalty to a headman - the Spaniards who came in the sixteenth century found no larger political grouping (only in the southern main island of Mindanao had Islam found a foothold in the fifteenth century).

Unlike the earth-bound societies of mainland East Asia where the village, with its ancestral graves, was the focus of tradition and collective loyalty, the barangay was built around a leader and his followers (the word refers originally to the sailing boat in which the Filipinos' Malay forebears had migrated to the archipelago). Chieftains traded, fought local wars, took captives in slave raids, and tattooed their bodies in proportion to their prowess in battle. The Spaniards simply superimposed themselves on these primitive oligarchies, governing through their accustomed chieftains who came to make up the colonial principalia. This local elite nominated town officials whose tenures were then confirmed by the central government in Manila. Spanish colonialism modified - but did not transform - the essentially riverine Malay

society. Catholicism coexisted easily with the older animism. The early Filipinos worshipped in sacred groves, caves or rock formations, but they had some conception of the Supreme Being who created the universe and ruled men. The rituals and pageantry of the Church all found parallels in the indigenous cults. To the Catholic custom of ritual co-parenthood - the compadrazgo - the early Filipinos took avidly, as a way of bringing their extended kinships into the circle of Christianity. The traditional Spanish concept that the exercise of power constitutes its own legitimacy bolstered similar concepts in the indigenous society. So did the Castilian lack of social cohesion in the traditional culture.

The communally owned land the Spaniards consolidated into royal estates, land grants to favored settlers, and friar estates. By the nineteenth century, the Philippines had a large, indigenous landed oligarchy - not so much Spanish as Chinese mestizo - who grew rich from the rise in world demand for tropical cash crops like sugar, copra, tobacco, and abaca. The opening of the colony to world commerce produced a classic dual economy. An enclave of export-crop production controlled by the landed gentry flourished alongside a large subsistence sector and a smaller food-crop commercial sector. Philippine latifundia have no counterparts in East Asia. The elite valued the prestige attached to the possession of land in Hispanic societies, even though the land was unproductive. By 1903, barely one percent of all the farms covered two-fifths of all the cultivated land - and even this did not reflect the entire picture because many rich families had scattered holdings in different parts of the town, province, or region on which they held sway.

From its colonial rulers, the Philippine State also inherited a weak civil service coupled with strong political awareness even among the poorest Filipino communities. Unlike the British, the Dutch or the French but like the Spaniards before them the Americans never developed a colonial bureaucracy. Instead of administrative capacity, they emphasized electoral politics in their Pacific colony. One of the first things they did was to expand the severely limited franchise set up by the Spaniards. The Partido Nacionalista, founded in 1907, is Southeast Asia's oldest political party. But by initally restricting suffrage to Filipinos of wealth, education, and previous government service, the American regime enabled the existing elites to preserve their dominant positions in local communities.

Early on, the civil service became just another prize of the spoils system. Then it became the employer of last resort: in 1993, the bureaucracy's payrolls encompassed eleven percent of all the country's workpeople.

In the bureaucratic states of East Asia, civil service rules and precedents are the civic norm. In the personalist Philippine political culture, by contrast, to be influential is to be privileged. It is to be exempt from the restraints the bureaucracy imposes on ordinary people - just as the principalia had been exempt from the Spanish tribute and forced labor.

In every East Asian newly-industrializing country, the capitalist-commercial class was relatively weak - in relation to the State - when the drive for development began. The Philippines is the exception. Its economic system is more Latin American than East Asian in the way it has concentrated land, industrial wealth, and political power in relatively few families. This elite, owing to its masterly opportunism and its remarkable openness to newcomers from below, has been able to preserve itself through every vicissitude the country has endured these past hundred years.

Throughout East Asia, strong nationalistic states united their peoples behind their economic goals, took direction of the market mechanisms and produced unprecedented - as well as widely-distributed - growth. In this country, the weakness of the State enabled personages, families, and clans of influence to use their privileged access to the machinery of government to extract unearned income from the economy.

POLITICIZATION AND INEQUALITY

The elite's competition for privileges through the law-making process, presidential power, and bureaucratic access has resulted in the widespread politicization of national society. It has also generated relatively high inequality. The income ratio between the richest fifth of the population is about 1:14, compared to the East Asian average of 1:9. Inequality has also inhibited the growth of medium-scale industries, which have, in a place like Taiwan, spurred industrial innovation and adaptability to market demand. In 1991, a mere ten corporations accounted for 26 percent of all the revenues; 40 percent of all the net income, and 34 percent of the total assets of the top one thousand Philippine corporations.

The Philippines had the misfortune of becoming independent in 1946 at a time when State interventionism was seen - from the example of the Soviet Union - as the way to both economic growth and social justice. Five-Year Plans were then fashionable: agriculture was seen as "backward" and industry as "modern." The country was among the first to go for capital-intensive, import-substitution industrialization; and it persisted in this basic policy despite the export opportunities of the 1960s and even the 1970s. As in Latin America, the State in the Philippines had

just as dominant a role as the East Asian developmental State. But its dominance was exercised in favor of the landed and the oligarchic class rather than on behalf of the entrepreneurial middle class responsible for much capitalist development. Thus it preserved a social order centered on privilege, and an economic system that was not so much capitalist as mercantilist and quasi-feudal.

The accretion of vested interests around the protectionist policies adopted in the postwar period imprisoned the Philippine State in one kind of economic policy, and prevented it from progressing to a higher industrial stage. Initially, the country seems to have stumbled into import-substitution industrialization in the wake of a foreign-exchange crisis in 1949. But, as in Latin America, the closed economy reinforced the traditional patronage system by multiplying the opportunities for rent-seeking from the business benefits that Government became able to bestow.

After an initial spurt of growth in the early 1950s, manufacturing slumped again in the middle 1960s as soon as it had exhausted the easier phases of import-substitution and reached the limit of the small home-market. Because the "infant" industries failed to mature, they could not increase their share of employment. Manufacturing's share of the work force actually declined from about 12 percent in the 1960s to about 11 percent in 1996. By comparison, 44 percent are still working as farmers, fishermen, hunters and forestry workers. Over the twenty years 1970-89, for instance eleven million workers were added to the work-force. Of these, only eight hundred thousand found jobs in manufacturing. Workers pushed out of overcrowded agriculture were absorbed not in manufacturing or in other industry but into petty commerce and other services equivalent to big-city underemployment. Others have migrated to overseas contract work in the Middle East, the United States, and in the booming economies of East Asia. There are some four million overseas Filipino workers in over one hundred and twenty countries, whose repatriated earnings - averaging 5 to 6 billion US dollars a year - keep the country's current account deficit manageable.

THE PROBLEM AND THE PROMISE OF THE ECONOMY

Felix Duero, a forty seven year-old laborer in a barrio of Laguna province, southeast of Metro Manila, earns 100 pesos ($ 3) every day that he works on a neighbor's farm. In the social hierarchy of the rural Philippines, he is among the lowliest of the low. His employer is himself the tenant of a retired school teacher in Pila town. Given a surplus of workhands and a shortage of land in this part of Luzon island, many tenants have become renters themselves. Hiring people like Felix Duero to work their holdings, they then become carpenters, small traders, town hall clerks, or even overseas contract workers. Duero's absentee employer drives a hauling truck cross-country between Saudi Arabia and Jordan.

Duero's father lost his own leasehold after contracting tuberculosis, which killed him at 58. Because Felix had dropped out of primary school after only three years - "I just lost interest" - he can barely read or write. So he cannot qualify for an assembly-line job in the light industries rising in Laguna. Only twenty five kilometers westward from where he grubs for a living is located the International Rice Research Institute responsible for monsoon Asia's Green Revolution - but it might well be a world away for all Felix Duero knows. Dark and small, eyes deep-set in a high cheekboned face, he weeds between the rice rows, his feet in the mud from first light till sunset, six months in the year. He has five children and his wife raises free-range chickens for the organic kitchens of Manila yuppies. Economic growth in the Philippines has iro-

nically pauperized landless peasants like Felix Duero. Beneath the brash business, political and professional middle class that runs Metro Manila and the large cities, lies a huge underclass kept down by poverty, illiteracy, and lack of marketable skills. One-third of Filipino school children still drop out of the primary-school cycle. Easily preventable diseases like measles, pneumonia and diarrheas still kill them in large numbers. Using 1991 official data, the economist Arsenio Balisacan calculated that thirty two out of every hundred Filipinos subsist on less than two thousand calories the Philippine considers to be the average minimum requirement: thirteen are barely above this food threshold and eleven are marginally poor. The Congressional Planning and Budget Office estimated that in 1994 almost eighty six out of every hundred agricultural families lived below the official poverty level. Rural migrants escaping the stagnant villages have turned many parts of Metro Manila into slums. By the year 2000, half of all Metro Manila's population will be squatters from the provinces.

"Philippine poverty is overwhelmingly a rural problem," said the World Bank in a November 1995 document. In Japan, Taiwan and South Korea,

Jeepneys, the famous collective taxis of the Philippines.

Rice paddies in Batangas.

agricultural modernization started off by land reform became the foundation of the new industry. In Indonesia, farm products growing by 4.2 percent yearly between 1976 and 1984 - the highest in East and Southeast Asia - enabled the Suharto regime to beat back poverty, according to the economist Harry T. Oshima. Thailand has become an agricultural superpower - exporting cassava root, tropical fruits, orchids and vegetables. Only the Philippine economy still carries on its back the burden of the rural poor.

Fifty years after independence, the Philippines has yet to shift from an agricultural to an industrial economy. Because financial policy has encouraged capital-intensive industry, its capacity to generate jobs is highly limited. For instance, the 506 industrial projects worth $12.42 billion registered by the Board of Investments from January to September 1994 are expected to produce only 93,026 jobs. Yet some eight hundred thousand young Filipinos enter the work force every year.

THE PROCESS OF POVERTY

Like most monsoon peoples, Filipinos had been accustomed to think of their land as limitless in its bounty: "throw a stick on the ground and it will grow." But only a fifth of the archipelago's thirty million hectares of territory is actually good farmland. Flood plains best suited for wet-rice culture make up only one and a half million hectares. There is no tradition of husbandry. While the sixteenth-century settlers of Central Luzon grew rice both in swiddens and in rain-fed fields, the Spaniards found them using neither draft animals nor plows. By then the Chinese had been fertilizing their bunded fields with oil-cake, fish meal, and beancurd waste for over a thousand years. Even now, less than a third of all the 2.3 million hectares planted to rice is irrigated and infrastructure-building has been devastated by the country's financial crisis. In 1994, the money actually released for irrigation was less than a fifth of the budget proposed by the National Irrigation Administration. As a result, the country averaged barely 2.8 metric tons of rice per hectare (in 1993), compared with 4.4 in Indonesia and six in China. Habits of profligacy about land-use persist, although the population has multiplied ten times over the last hundred years. Every year, the Philippines has 1.3 million more mouths to feed. It exhausted its last land frontier in the 1960s.

The Philippines seems more Latin American than East Asian in its land-tenure system. As late as 1980, only three percent of all farms were larger than ten hectares, but they accounted for about a quarter of all farm land. Redistributive agrarian reform - which has gone on since 1972 - has been "disappointingly slow; financing the programme has been a major constraint," said an Asian Development Bank study.

The transition from colonialism did not weaken the landed oligarchy in the least. It shifted effortlessly to import-substitution industrialization in the 1950s. Industry - typically large-scale and capital intensive - is still concentrated in Metro Manila and its environs. But industry never absorbed the excess workers from agriculture, as the conventional wisdom then thought it would. An overvalued peso in fact encouraged "progressive" farmers to "modernize" by using tractors and mechanical threshers. Meanwhile, tariff walls and restrictions on imported industrial products reduced the relative price of farm products and raised the cost of imported fertilizers. Landless peasants like Felix Duero provided the cannon-fodder for two successive Communist insurgencies led by radical intellectuals in 1950-53 and again in 1969-87. But these rebellions ebbed without a lasting impact on the social order.

Today, more and more Filipino leaders recognize their country's need for decentralized, rural-based industrialization that eases poverty and income inequality and gives ordinary people a stake in their country's development. Senator Edgardo J. Angara, a Vice-Presidential candidate in 1998, says, "Aggregate growth is not enough: development must improve the lot of the masses of the people and enable them to share in an economy that becomes structurally and technologically richer."

Dried fish is a native favorite of the Filipinos.

135

The economist Romeo Bautista notes that even "accelerated agricultural growth will not suffice; as the country's experience between 1965 and 1980 showed, it does not necessarily lead to rapid growth of the national economy that is equitable and sustainable." That cycle of growth - because it benefited disproportionately the rural elite - dissipated itself in a splurge on imported goods. It did not generate the rural industry and off-farm jobs that the same kind of growth did for Taiwan at roughly the same time.

But countries cannot just walk away from mistakes in economic planning. Every policy - right or wrong - generates its train of consequences; and the protectionist, anti-agriculture policies of the Philippines has followed over the last thirty years have produced their own entrenched interests. Over the last fifteen years, agricultural productivity has actually been growing more slowly than the population. Rice production in 1995 fell short of its target of 11.5 million tons by nine hundred thousand tons and caused a food crisis which triggered double-digit inflation and some political unrest.

It is clear that Philippine agriculture must diversify from the traditional rice, corn, sugar and coconuts to a larger assortment of crops, animals, fish and forest products if it is to absorb more workhands, boost nutrition levels, reduce income disparities and raise demands at home for the products of industry. Promoting high-value crops is a major plank in the government program of Speaker Jose de Venecia, whom President Ramos has endorsed as his successor. The few big farming corporations are shifting to high-value crops: fruits, root crops, vegetables, spices and condiments, and ornamentals. Poultry and meat growers are popularizing contract agriculture but the bulk of rural workpeople are still yoked to subsistence farming.

DUAL POLITICS AT ODDS WITH ITSELF

The marxists believe that politics merely expresses the economic power-relations in a community. The country's dual politics - one "traditional", the other "new" - does seem to to reflect the distortions of an economy shaped by the colonial experience.

The two halves of the country's dual economy are still linked only tenuously: cheap food and cheap workhands being the main commodities from the subsistence sector that the modern sector needs. And the gap between the two halves is both huge and increasing. Average incomes in the municipality of Makati - Metro Manila's managerial and financial center - are nine times larger than those in the poorest province, Northern Samar in the Eastern Visayas.

This lopsided economic base holds up the superstructure of national politics - which is also split into two unequal halves. Its traditional part is founded on relationships of mutual dependence between "little people" and "big people" in the small-scale community. In exchange for the local patron's protection and material help, those who receive his beneficence give him their deference and their votes. Meanwhile, the relatively modern sector of the economy has nurtured social forces outside the patronage system. Of these groups, the most important is the city middle class of business people, professionals, army officers, civil servants, office workers and university students. Twelve years ago, it made the peaceful "People Power" revolution that overthrew the caudillo Ferdinand E. Marcos. The middle class commonly complains about the enduring hold of patronage politics on both local and national administrations. The truth is that national society is changing in both its economic base and in its political and social superstructure. The two halves of the dual economy are being painfully united into one national economy. The cash nexus is increasingly replacing the face-to-face transactions of the old society. Social and economic structures are based less and less on communal values shared by rich and poor people. The decline of agriculture is also eroding the influence of the once-decisive rural vote; and national "talk" radio and television are passing down urban political opinion to their rural audiences.

In national politics, new-style factions are replacing the old ones. Only in a few predominantly rural, relatively isolated areas can traditional patrons still deliver large blocs of vote. For the old factions, politics had been merely one outlet for the social competition among leading local families. The new factions are specialized electoral machines - based less on family ties, personal loyalties, and mutual obligation than on the frank exchanges of votes for money and other material favors. New-type politicians, too, are coming up; and these are more and more self-made men and women rather than mere inheritors of some honored local name. This trend harks back to the Spanish and the pre-colonial Filipino tradition of a "spontaneous democracy" which offers a place in the sun for all those strong enough to take it. President Ramos - a professional soldier who graduated from the U.S. Military Academy at West Point in 1950 as a Philippine Government scholar and who retired Chief of Staff in 1988 - represents these new politicians who increasingly enter national politics not from the local machines but from careers in business, the higher professions, and the senior civil service.

The Makati skyline in Metro Manila.

Change - once it begins - is often outpaced by people's expectations. Since 1986, the middle class has become increasingly assertive in national politics. Its spokesmen - religious and civic leaders, journalists, academic intellectuals, unionists and the organizers of non-government and people's organizations as well as ambitious "new politicians" - have kept up their attacks on the traditional politicians, whom they call "trapos" - "rags."

Traditionally, the Philippine Church has preached a Latin-American type of religiosity - of personal piety separate from social responsibility. Since the Second Vatican Council (1962) however, some bishops, priests and nuns have become increasingly active participants in the political debate. In fact, at the height of the New People's Army rebellion, a radical Church grouping adopted not only the Maoist Communist party's social analysis of the Philippine condition but also the violent solution it proposed. Nowadays the Bishops Conference routinely pronounces the Philippine Church's stand on political questions as they arise. These pronouncements are sometimes blunted by the ambiguity of doctrine on the Church's role in secular life. This comparative blandness of the Bishops Conference probably explains the high visibility of the outspoken Jaime Cardinal Sin, whose political influence extends well beyond his archdiocese of Manila. But because eighty-three percent of all Filipinos are nominally Catholic, there is no "Catholic vote." Filipinos are ambivalent about the Church's participation in national politics, and the hierarchy's interventionism mobilizes support only when it comes down on a political issue that people already feel deeply about.

Middle-class impatience with the traditional politics is matched by increasing despair among the poorest Filipinos. The breakdown of client-patron relationships has made the lives of tenant families less and less secure. But, ironically, there is little alienation or rejection of the electoral system. Opinion surveys analyzed by the Jesuit John J. Carroll, an American social scientist of the Ateneo University in Metro Manila, still confirm the tendency of the Filipino poor, of the less educated and of rural people in general "simply to voice approval of the system and for the authority figures within it." Politics for them is a spectacle, but

Pineapple plantation in Mindanao.

they do not expect its outcome to change their lives.* The middle class feels most keenly the sense of national humiliation at being overtaken in the race for growth by neighbors it has always regarded as somehow inferior. It remembers how easily, in 1986, it was able to force through an extra constitutional change of government. But its persistent efforts to elect an administration of "non-politicians" are liable to be frustrated by the one-man-one-vote system which favors the rural and urban-slum machines.

The saying that all politics is local is nowhere more true than it is in the Philippines. Until now, national political parties have been organized from the bottom up- jerry-built from factions operating at town or province level - and whose party allegiances shift depending on their basic interests: stay in power and share in the spoils of office. Voters' loyalty depends less on an official's policies as on the public-works projects he is able to obtain for his constituency, and on the particularistic help he is able to give. Fr. Carroll notes: "One's Congressman is seen primarily as a social welfare institution - which of course encourages him to act as such in the interest of re-election." The highly-factionalized character of national politics - a legacy of both Malay and Spanish cultures - contrasts with the disciplined, and highly centralized

parties in Taiwan, Singapore and South Korea. Philippine parties are "catch-all" groupings - inclusive, non-ideological, pragmatic - seeking the support of all sectors and all social and income groups. Indistinguishable in their policies and in their bases of support, they do not reflect the social and ideological cleavages in national society. The American political scientist, Carl Lande, argues that because the Philippine parties have been unable to resolve critical social issues democratically, grave social conflicts such as the decades of tenant grievances in Central Luzon and "Christian" encroachments on ancestral lands of the Muslim minority in Mindanao and Sulu have moved outside the parliamentary arena and burst out in open insurgency and secessionism.

The breakdown of the two-party system under the 1987 Constitution's injunction that a "free and open party system should be allowed to develop" has produced parties that are merely the vehicles of personal ambition and a proliferation of candidates. Seven of them contested the presidency in 1992, which General Ramos won with only 24 percent of the vote, the first elected minority president in national history - and probably four or five will do so in 1998. This plurality of candidates also reflects an electorate diversifying into single-issue interests. The prospect now is of more "minority Presidents" running administrations backed by perpetually-shifting legislative coalitions - with all its implications for political instability and improvised public policies.

Voters tend to focus on personalities rather on policies. In recent times, this has resulted in a spate of radio, television, film, and sports personalities being elected to local governments and the legislature. The Senate has a former film actor who boasts his possession of an amulet, two TV hosts, and a basketball star among its twenty four members. The leading candidate in the May 1998 presidential election, Vice-President Joseph Estrada, was for many years an actor in roles that showed him as "willing to stand up and fight for the poor." Regionalism too is still a powerful political emotion. Except among the relatively cosmopolitan Tagalog of Manila and its surrounding provinces, voters invariably support candidates for national office who speak their language and identify with their home region. And these language-group loyalties remain strong even when their speakers migrate to other regions, since it is their language alone that gives them their unique identity and sense of solidarity.

WHAT REFORMS HAVE ACCOMPLISHED SO FAR

By President Ramos' own reckoning, one hundred and fifty nine major reform laws have been enacted by the legislative coalition supporting his Philippines 2000 program. Sixty-three of these laws deal with economic reform, fifty seven with social reform and thirty eight with political reform. The new economic laws include an innovative "build-operate-transfer" law that enables private business to invest in electric-power plants, toll highways, mass-transit systems, and other overhead capital. In December 1997, Congress finished overhauling the tax system to make it progressive (at the moment, high-income business taxpayers can deduct as much as 92 percent of their gross income) and to enable it to finance adequately the costs of social reform and national modernization. Its passage into law will enable the country to exit from thirty five years of continuous financial supervision and discipline by the International Monetary Fund.

The opening of the economy has made the country's skilled, adaptable, and English-speaking work people attractive to migratory capital from the industrial countries (Filipino workers were rated Asia's most competitive labor pool by senior executives throughout the region in a September 1997 survey by the Hong Kong-based Political and Economic Risk Consultancy). In 1997, the country experienced a surge in investments that multiplied nine times over the 1996 totals. A full third came from the West - the biggest chunks from France, Britain, and the United States - and it was distributed among the

sixty five "growth zones" outside Metropolitan Manila. The most popular of these export platforms are the former American naval base at Subic and airbase at Clark Field, both in Luzon. The five provinces directly south of Manila have become one large growth zone acronymed CALABARZON. General Santos City in southern Mindanao, facing Borneo and the spice islands of Eastern Indonesia, has become an air-sea hub for the farm-products of the high Mindanao plateau and the tuna harvests of the Sulu Sea. For Japanese investors, the most favored destination is Mactan in Cebu, the second-largest city.

In recent years the Philippines has been a leading destination of foreign investments in information technology. Intel, Motorola, Oracle, Texas Instruments, Seagate, Fujitsu, Amkor-Anam, Nippon Electronic, Taiwan's Acer, Cypress have all staked out Philippine plants; and electronics now make up half of all the country's exports.

The country's economic managers expect the Uruguay Round agreements (which the Senate has ratified) to generate one hundred and fourteen thousand net jobs - against the loss of eleven thousand jobs in declining sectors of the economy. The economy must continue to grow by at least 6 percent a year if it is to continue generating new jobs. More than one million new jobs a year are needed to wipe out the backlog of the unemployed as well as to absorb the eight hundred thousand young people who enter the work force yearly. Because of the currency turmoil, the Ramos technocrats have scaled down their forecasts for GNP growth in 1997 from 7.5 percent to 5.5 percent. In 1996, GNP grew by 6.8 percent.

The recommendations of a Congressional Commis-sion on Agricultural Modernization have just been signed into law. They are expected to focus Government responsibility for agriculture, which is now spread among at least five Cabinet offices, into the Department of Agriculture. The review is also expected to result in more money for agriculture research - on which the Philippines now spends the least among all the ASEAN countries. The basic need is for Government to redress the price bias against agriculture in trade and industrial policy and to discriminate in favor of rural-based industries and enterprises because the social desirability or rural-based production exceeds its private profitability. The recommendations also urge Government to improve small farmers' access to irrigation water, credit, fertilizer, and other resources by redistributing land-holdings through an effective agrarian reform program, and by promoting small-scale, labor-intensive agricultural production and processing.

Despite successive agrarian-reform programs, inequality in landholding actually worsened over the generation between 1960 and 1991. Land reform has hardly affected sugar and coconut lands, where land distribution is most unequal. Nearly ten years after the Comprehensive Agrarian Reform Program was passed in 1988, the two Cabinet departments managing it have disposed of only a little more than half of the lands they are supposed to redistribute. Among the problems that beset the program, the inadequacy of funds with which to buy privately-owned lands is the most serious. By the end of 1996, the Agrarian Reform Fund had run through 48.7 billion pesos. An additional 100 billion pesos will probably be needed to complete the program. Yet it is not enough to redistribute land: if land reform is to succeed, beneficiaries must be helped to make their farms productive - with irrigation, technology and credit.

The future of Philippine agriculture hinges on two basic trends - the growing number of mouths to feed and decreasing arable land. Today's seventy million Filipinos will become one hundred and twenty million in 23 years' time. Meanwhile, urbanization (close to six out of every ten Filipinos now live in cities) and environmental degradation will be putting tremendous pressure on land tenure systems. Unavoidably, future agriculture will consist of small farms tilled by the owners themselves. This pattern will determine wich technologies will be used, the products favored, and the supporting institutions that will emerge. Intensive cultivation will be the norm. Future Filipino farmers will be professionals and not hired hands like Felix Duero. Like European agriculturists, they will be tillers by choice, who depend on high productivity and innovative marketing to support middle-class lifestyles.

THE FUTURE OF POLITICS AND THE ECONOMY

Discoursing on East Asia's currency turmoil before European industrialists, traders, and businessmen in Hong Kong in October 1997, President Ramos termed the financial crisis as less of a psychological turning point on the region's path of high growth than a "wake-up call" for its high-fliers. The expert opinion is that the Asian "currency crises of 1997 are not the sign of the end of the Asian growth but rather a recurring - if difficult to predict - pattern of financial instability that often accompanies rapid economic growth." Like many other economists, Steven Radelet and Jeffrey Sachs of Harvard expect the regional economies to return to rapid growth within two-three years and East Asia to reemerge as the world's center of economic activity after giving way to the West beginning in the early 1500s. The export-growth strategy should continue to work as East Asia still is a primary destination of migratory capital fleeing high labor-cost countries in the West. Even the Japanese are moving more and more of their industrial production sites offshore. Radelet and Sachs estimate that by 2025, Asia will account for 55-60 percent of world income, with the West's relative share falling from around 45 percent in 1997 to anywhere between 20-30 percent.

The lesson President Ramos himself reads from the currency turmoil is that "globalization has become a fact of life, and that global markets punish policy mistakes severely. Growing interdependence means that economic problems in one country could reecho in other economies; and the remedy lies not in turning away from the world but in embracing it even more closely." Not only is the Philippines resolving the weaknesses in its financial system. It is also sharpening its competitive edge, in a continuing effort to bring the country into the mainstream of global competition.

A "pole-vaulting strategy" Ramos initiated in early 1997 would ride on the strengths of the country's East Asian neighbors and optimize the country's distinct advantages - which lie in its open society, its strategic location and archipelagic setting; its adaptable workpeople and its lead in such new-type industries as health and medical services, education, accountancy and management, as well as information and knowledge-based technologies. Filipino managers are prized regionwide for their skills and their ability to adapt to other cultures, their loyalty and their inclination to work hard.

Industries in which the Philippines has potential export winners include electronics, garments, furniture, seaweeds and caragheenan, fresh fruits and motor vehicles and components. Transnational managers emphasize the crucial importance of the country's human capital to its competitiveness: ironically, the Philippines, among all the ASEAN states, has historically spent the least on basic education. Reform of the education system and the nurturing particularly of scientists, engineers and managers have been promised by Speaker de Venecia, President Ramos's nominated successor.

Despite rising costs because of the de facto devaluation of the peso, stiffer competition from China and its other neighbors, and the country's lack of infrastructure, the Philippines continues to be regarded as a prime investment site. A December 1997 survey of transnationals in the country - by the London-based Economist Intelligence - found 73 percent of them drawing up expansion programs over the next three years. President Ramos's ultimate goal is to assert the rule of law: to stop political arbitrariness, to end the dominance of the influential and to establish the social and legal equality that characterizes the working democracy. To achieve this goal, Mr. Ramos has come to realize he must first raise the political capacity of the administrative machinery. Increasing political capacity means increasing the legitimacy and effectiveness of State institutions - of the bureaucracy most of all; of the police; the judiciary; the legislature. Measured against the best of the Asian "tiger" economies, the fragility of Philippine political institutions is plain to see - in laws that are enforced indifferently in a tax effort that is the lowest in ASEAN; in the persistence of private armies and the prevalence of crime; in the corruptibility of portions of the judiciary. Raising political capacity must also mean infusing a minimum set of standards - of personal integrity, efficiency, national spirit - in those who direct the affairs of the State. President Ramos has therefore identified effective government as the first requisite to the country's modernization.

Most urgently, this means streamlining the civil service: ending Government's role as the employer of last resort, setting up a professional career-officer corps, and raising public-sector salaries to near equality with those of modern industry. The legislature refuses to grant Mr. Ramos the authority he has sought for emergency powers to reorganize the bureaucracy. Piecemeal reform of the most economically sensitive agencies has already managed to cut the costs of doing business. In March 1997, the Hong Kong-based Political and Economic Risk Consultancy reported a reduction in Philippine Government red tape - raising the country to fourth rank among the regional economies in terms of bureaucratic efficiency.

Jose T. Almonte, President Ramos's national security adviser and general-purpose intellectual, argues that many of the country's problems are caused not by design or wrongdoing but by the simple lack of State capability. "Because we have not yet institutionalized the rule of law, officials are able to act discretionally." The retired general's critics invariably represent Almonte's periodic calls for a "stronger" Philippine state as plots to impose a military dictatorship. But Almonte argues that the clear and present danger

Houses on stilts in Tawi-Tawi (Sulu Archipelago).

in the developing countries is not so much totalitarianism as society's relapse into social anarchy. Almonte has also warned against complacency on Government's part - emphasizing that only the "easy" reforms have been accomplished so far, and that as the "hard" reforms requiring greater administrative capacity are attempted, "the weaknesses of the Philippine state are starting to show." In recent months, the Ramos Administration's difficulties have been exacerbated by decisions on economic questions by a conservative Supreme Court which reversed the Executive Branch's decision to deregulate the oil industry and asserted the outmoded "Filipino First" policy in striking down the privatization of the landmark Manila Hotel.

Political Reform is one of these "hard" tasks. The basic problem is the weakness of the party system - which has prevented it from offering meaningful policy choices - and so to provide for orderly political change. The struggles and intrigues among political caudillos have left unresolved national society's political cleavages. Historically, the deepest and widest of these has been the gulf between the landed and the landless in the country's heartland of Central Luzon. But today, resentments against an "Imperial Manila" is intensifying in the other regions - particularly in the Visayas, in Muslim Mindanao, the tribal Cordilleras, and even the Bicol region in southern Luzon, all areas that feel relatively neglected by the central Government. Exporters too had been chafing at a peso overpriced to benefit national manufacturers; and there are strains between the few large industries and the many small-and-medium ones.

Fortunately, the country harbors no hereditary political hatreds. As Carl Lande has noted, Filipinos have little class consciousness in the Marxist sense: instead of seeking solidarity with others in their predicament, they tend to seek individual and family upward social mobility.

Fr. Carroll suggests that the future of Philippine democracy "lies outside the formally political arena; it lies in what is coming to be called civil society." He speculates that the labor unions, peasants' organizations, urban-poor organizations, basic Christian communities, parent-teachers' organizations, the churches and all the other mediating institutions between the individual and the state can become the building blocks of "true political parties based on principles and programs."

The reorientation of politics away from political personalities toward strong and programmatically-distinct parties has barely begun. But some observers find hope in the gradual increase - particularly in the House of Representatives - of modern issue-oriented politicians. And many Filipinos - contemplating the rising political troubles in some of their faster-growing neighbor-countries - console themselves with the thought that their country has at least already come through its democratic revolution.

THE FUTURE OF PHILIPPINE DEMOCRACY

What the Philippines has set out to do - to develop as a democracy - goes against the grain of the conventional wisdom in East Asia. The dominant view is that democracy and development cannot go together "because the exuberance of unrestrained democracy leads to undisciplined and disorderly conditions inimical to development." But authoritarianism is unworkable for a half-modern, half-feudal society like the Philippines - which is modern enough for people to demand their political rights but feudal enough for many of our politicians to treat government as merely a way of distributing patronage.

Even as they consolidate their economic gains, Filipinos are beginning to look beyond economic growth to the modernization of their country. More and more they realize that modernization is not merely about expanding the economy and accumulating material goods. Modernization properly means people sharing a belief and commitment in how society should be ordered: for what purpose and for whose benefit. Modernization also means raising the political capabilities of the State to free it once and for all from the influence of self-seeking economic oligarchies and political dynasties. It also means the elected leaders becoming fully accountable to the governed. It means both empowering ordinary people and awakening the well-to-do to their social conscience. Finally, modernization also means civic responsibility and democratization. It means the country's business becoming the business of every citizen.

In a sense, modernizing the way today's Filipinos are trying to do is modernizing the "hard way." The Philippine State accepts ground rules, restraints, handicaps that other East Asian governments do not. Philippine democracy may be far from perfect, but it seems to work well enough for it to improve the Filipino's situation incrementally. Given the lack of disciplined political parties and a clear majority in the Legislature, governing must be by informal coalitions such as President Ramos has organized with the moderate opposition in Congress and the "social pacts" he has negotiated with business, the professions, organized workers, religious groups and people's organizations.

People now generally accept that there are many paths to a working representative system. If democracy in America revolves around individual rights, Western

Roses from France are cultivated in
Luzon by French horticulture engineers.

European states emphasize a greater degree of
social responsibility. The political scientist Francis
Fukuyama has suggested that Confucian cultures
could generate more group-oriented types of demo-
cracies - such as Japan's - in order to moderate the
atomizing individualism inherent in traditional indi-
vidualist doctrine. In the Philippines, the problem is
how to reconcile the democratic ideology most
Filipinos subscribe to with a cultural tradition founded on hierarchical relationships between "big
people" and "small people" and where oligarchic
power still coexists with mass poverty.

As President Ramos has noted again and again,
the kind of democracy Filipinos have known for
the better part of this century has emphasized the
individual over the community: private gain over the
public good and civic rights over civic duties.

Freedom by itself does not bring about progress.
Filipinos know all too well how easily political power
without accountability can lead to despotism and
plunder. Freedom without responsibility can result in
a noisy minority overwhelming the silent majority.
Filipinos see their salvation not in curtailing their
democracy but in enlarging it - by devolving political
authority from the center in Manila to local governments throughout the archipelago; and by encouraging ordinary Filipinos to use their votes and their
organizational strength to ensure that their wants,
needs and hopes are really heard in the making of
public policy.

FOOTNOTES

The section on politics benefited greatly from monographs by Brigadier General Jose
T. Almonte (Ret.), Presidential Security Adviser; John J. Carroll, S.J.; and by Carl H.
Lande. Fr. Carroll's paper, "Glimpses into Philippine Political Culture: Gleanings from
the Ateneo Public Opinion Survey Data," appeared in Pilipinas, No. 22, Spring 1994.
Lande's "The 1992 Philippine Presidential Election: A Geographic and Statistical
Analysis," is an unpublished manuscript. Fr. Carroll is Director of the Institute on
Church and Social Issues at the Ateneo University. General Almonte's paper was deli-
vered before the Foreign Correspondents' Association of the Philippines in Manila on 21
January, 1998.

The Filipino novel in English and its roots

by Cristina Pantoja Hidalgo

CRISTINA PANTOJA HIDALGO received her education from the University of Santo Tomas (Bachelor of Philosophy, magna cum laude), where she began her writing and teaching career. She holds a Ph. D. in Comparative Literature and, currently, a professorship at the University of the Philippines. She is coordinator of the University's Creative Writing program, an associate of the prestigious U.P. Creative Writing Center. Mrs. Hidalgo has authored some fourteen books of travel, literary criticism and fiction, including Recuerdo: A Novel which won the Carlos Palanca Grand prize in 1996. She was the recipient of the Manila Critic's Award for Fiction (for Tales for a Rainy Night) and co-edited Philippine Post-Colonial Studies (1993) and The Likhaan Book of Poetry and Fiction 1995 (1996).

INTRODUCTION

In 1965, Leonidas Benesa complained that when he was asked to prepare a paper on the Filipino novel in English from 1941 to 1962 he had to spend the greater part of the five weeks given him on a *"frantic expedition that looked more archeological than historico-literary."* At the end of it, he had come up with only eleven novels published in those thirty years. Thirty-five years later, the situation is quite different. Before writing this paper, I put together a list of novels published in the last thirty years.[1]

In the sixties and seventies, during the upsurge of the student-led militant nationalist movement, several critics took the position that Philippine literature in English, being elitist, alienated, divorced from reality, and a tool of imperialism, could never be an appropriate vehicle for Filipino emotions and aspirations. A less extremist position was that, while English was a legitimate medium of self-expression for bourgeois writers who had been educated in English, literature in English was a minor part of Philippine literature, and would soon be totally eclipsed by literature in Filipino. There has been no lack of writers and critics who have questioned the validity of both positions. I would simply suggest that a cursory examination of the above list would justify some skepticism. Certainly all thirty-nine novels are firmly grounded in Philippine realities, many of them in contemporary Philippine realities. It is not possible in a paper of this length to go into a discussion of each novel. But to mention just a few, in Joaquin's *Cave and Shadows*, Rosca's *State of War*, Gamalinda's *Empire of Memory*, Yuson's *The Great Philippine Jungle Energy Café*, Jose's *Viajero*, and Hidalgo's *Recuerdo*, myth, history, and current events intermingle, and different voices - reportorial, lyrical, satiric, ironic, rapturous - combine to weave tales at once romantic and realistic. Rosca's *Twice Blessed* focuses on a diabolic brother and sister who vividly recall Ferdinand and Imelda Marcos. Ty-Casper's *Awaiting Trespass*, *Dread Empire*, *A Small Party in the Garden* and *Wings of Stone*, Dalisay's *Killing Time in a Warm Place*, and Tiempo's *The Alien Corn* deal with the turbulence of the martial law period. Santos' two novels focus on the *Pinoy* in America. Chai's *The Last Time I Saw Mother* tackles the Filipino-Chinese experience. Tiempo's *One, Tilting Leaves* takes on environmental problems in Nueva Vizcaya. But even those novels that are set in an earlier time (Castillo's *The Firewalkers* and Salanga's *The Birthing of Hannibal Valdez* are set in the early years of the American colonial period. Tiempo's *The Standard Bearer*, Brainard's *Song of Yvonne* and Moore's *The Honey, the Locusts* take place during the Japanese occupation) cannot in any way be considered escapist or "aestheticist". Moreover,

all clearly take a clear anti-colonial (perhaps the better word is "post-colonial") position. I would even suggest that if the novel in English must be faulted, it would be for having the tendency to become a bit heavy-handed in "making its point." The point often has to do with healing wounds (the nation's as well as the individual's), and with the writer's possible role in this process. This is particularly true in the case of the most recent works, which are now being referred to as "martial law novels."

Perhaps the problem is the tendency to look at Philippine literature in English as though it were somehow autonomous, rather than part of a larger body of literary works written in several languages. In 1967, NVM Gonzales, fictionist, essayist, journalist, and professor of literature, wrote:

"A writer starting out in 1966 is not likely to pick up a tradition, or some thread of it, which his society has already become familiar with dating since, say, 1866. There just isn't any...or, maybe there is, but this hasn't been adequately described to be recognizable. Consciousness of it has not become part of our would-be writer's equipment. He is led to picking up what is of the moment and, international communication being what it is today, he is as likely to join forces with the Existentialist or the Beats, as... with the Sensualists."

At the time that Gonzales made those observations, literary scholars - the few who made Philippine Literature their field of specialization - tended to focus on literature in English as an independent, isolated body of work, with no links to either, on the one hand, the literatures written in Tagalog[2] and the other Philippine languages, or, on the other hand, with literature written in Spanish. *Philippine Literature from Ancient Times to the Present* (del Castillo & Medina 1966) was one of the few books in its time to attempt a literary history covering Philippine literature in Tagalog, Spanish and English. But it did not study relations or connections or trace influences. It merely recorded general trends and characteristics, listed important authors and works, and commented on them briefly. *Brown Heritage* (1967), edited by Antonio Manuod, was an impressive volume in that it was a first attempt to study literature in the context of Philippine culture in general, but the essays in it were rather uneven in quality.

Since then, literary scholarship has made some strides. In the introductory chapters of *Philippine Literature: a History and Anthology*, for example, Bienvenido and Cynthia Lumbera discuss literature in relation to the socio-economic and political history of the country. And *Origins and Rise of the Filipino Novel* traces the development of the novel from pre-Hispanic times to 1940, taking pains to demonstrate the interconnectedness of all the country's literatures.

Photo facing the title page
Coconut trees along the coast of Boracay.
Above
A small island off Sirgiao.

The subject of this essay is the novel, specifically the Filipino novel written in English, and it is my thesis that it is not in the least the strange species that it appeared to be when the Ateneo de Manila sponsored a series of lectures which eventually were collected in the book *Brown Heritage*. On the contrary, it belongs to a long and rich narrative tradition. Resil Mojares had already made this point in his groundbreaking study of the Philippine novel's origins. But his study stopped with the pre-war novel in English.[3] This essay is a modest start in the direction of updating his investigation.

The novel had been in existence for a while in Europe when it was "imported" into the Philippines. Jose Rizal, an *indio* (native) who had been partly educated in Europe, wrote what is regarded by some as the first Filipino novel, *Noli Me Tangere* (1887). However, the history of the Filipino novel does not begin with him. And while it is true that the novel in the Philippines was modeled after western prototypes, its roots are deep in native soil. There is a tradition of local narratives - oral epics, ballads, tales, and other folk narratives - to which were later added other narrative types introduced by the Spaniards, including metrical romances,

lives of saints, fables, parables, etc. The novel in the Philippines developed by combining elements from those different traditions. Naturally, this development was affected by social and political realities, the most important of which was colonialism.

That the literary history of the Philippines is a truncated one, *"marked by profound interruptions and interference,"* is glaringly obvious. The intrusion of Spain resulted in the decline of the folk epics, and the ascendancy of the *pasyon*, a folk epic of a sort, but a Christian one, and the *corrido*, the metrical romance. In places which remained isolated from the mainstream Hispanic culture, this displacement did not occur. There the epic persisted, in an inevitably altered fashion.

There is no direct link between these early narrative forms and the modern novel, but scholars like Mojares have demonstrated that there is clearly a connection between the epic and the *corrido*, and between the *corrido* and the religious conduct-books and the novel. With the rise of literacy and printing, prose came into its own, in the form of chronicles, conduct-books, historical reports, and, finally, the novel (initially written in Spanish by Spaniards and serialized in periodicals).

Any account of the novel in English in the Philippines, must therefore begin, not with Rizal, but with the ancient oral narratives. In this essay, I rely for my account of the novel's origins and early development on the excellent work done by Mojares and Lumbera.

BEGINNINGS

A native syllabary was in existence when the first Spaniards reached the islands in 1521, but scholars have now established that it was not used for either recording or producing songs and other imaginative works, which were part of oral traditions. Moreover, this syllabary fell into total disuse during the three centuries of Spanish rule.

Fortunately, in the last three decades, the epics, folk tales, legends, riddles and proverbs of different groups of Filipinos (material which, until the late sixties, was virtually unknown, particularly to people who grew up in the cities), have become accessible through the efforts of scholars/translators. The oral literatures of ancient Filipinos are rich in lyric poetry, but as this essay is focused on the novel, I shall briefly touch only on the early narratives, which influenced the development of prose in the different Philippine languages. Mojares claims that there are from 100 to 500 tales in the oral tradition of any Philippine culture, and *"as many as 1,000 tales in an unacculturated group."*

The epics are the most important of these oral narratives. In the eighties, as many as thirty had been identified: two from Christianized lowland groups - the Iluko *Lam-ang* and the Bicolano *Handiong*; six from the non-Christian hilltribes of Luzon, among them the Ifugao *Hudhud* and the Kalinga *Ullalim*; one from the Visayas - the *Hinilawod* of Central Panay; and at least five epics from Muslim Mindanao, like *Bantugan*, the Maranaw epic.[4]

On the significance of these epics for Philippine literature, Mojares writes:

"The extent to which folk life is permeated by the world of the epic cannot be overstressed. The epic is ubiquitous: it appears in the tribal repertoire of music plays on gongs and other instruments; it is invoked in proverbs and common prayers; it is expressed in various forms of folk drama; it is diffused in the broken-down forms of tales and ballads. It also guides social aspirations..."

In form, the Philippine epics are much like oral literature all over the world, containing conventions like formulaic repetitions, stereotyped characterization, rhythmic and musical devices, in short, conventions which facilitate oral transmission.

The epic of the Ilocanos, *Lam-ang*, is the most interesting for our purposes because, unlike the other epics, it is attributed to one author, Pedro Bukaneg, who is believed to have based his narrative on an old Itneg tale. It is also a hybrid work, combining "pagan" with Christian elements, *"poised between epic and romance."*

THE HISPANIC PERIOD

"Spanish colonial rule was supposed to derive its authority from the union of Church and State. The parish priest, however, was practically the only Spaniard who had direct contact with Filipinos... The literature of the entire period was in the main created under his encouragement and supervision."

For almost three centuries, the religious orders monopolized printing presses so that early written literature was entirely religious in content. The first book published in the Philippines was the *Doctrina Christiana* (1593). The first Filipino writers were the so-called *Ladino* (latinized) poets of the seventeenth century, young men who taught the friars the native languages and were also among the first natives to learn Spanish. They produced poems affirming Christian values, written in Spanish and Tagalog and using the Latin alphabet.

"Until the middle of the 19th century... literature was distinctly "medieval" in temper, using the term to refer to an intellectual orientation that is arealist and ahistorical and a scale of literary values that is romantic in its fixation with ideal norms, as expressed in the remote and patterned worlds of knights and saints, and didactic in its subordination of the narrative to the motive of instruction and illustration. This literary medievalism has its underpinnings in the character of the time."

With the arrival of the Spaniards and the rise of literacy, the epics and other types of oral literature declined, to be supplanted by the pasyon and the *corrido*.

Lumbera and Lumbera regard Gaspar Aquino de Belen as the *"first Filipino literary artist, the first one to come up with a long work that bore the signs of conscious design and careful composition"*. His *Ang Mahal na Passion ni Jesu Christong Panginoon Natin* (1704), written in Tagalog octosyllabic verse, narrates the events of Jesus' death, beginning with the Last Supper. It was sung to a fixed melody, much like the traditional epics had been, as part of Lenten season rituals. From it evolved what was to be called the *pasyon*, an account of the life of Christ, focusing on the passion and the crucifixion.

"It has a ubiquitous existence in our literary history: it appears as a printed text and has been called 'the Filipino bible'; it is read aloud or chanted during Lent (a practice called pabasa*); and it is dramatized on stage (in the* sinakulo, cenaculo[5]*)."*

There are versions of the *pasyon* among the nine major linguistic groups in Luzon and the Visayas, the oldest being the Iluko version, attributed to the

Village huts on the shores of Tawi-Tawi

Augustinian priest, Antonio Megia, and believed to have been written in 1621. According to the historian Rey Ileto, who has studied the *pasyon* as an alternative to mainstream history (which, he asserts, was written from the point of view of the bourgeois leadership of the Philippine Revolution), the most important of these different versions is the *Pasyong Pilapil* written in 1814.[6]

"Before the abolition of friar censorship by the republic and American colonial governments, the pasyon was one of the few literary works available to the rural population, and therefore could not fail to shape the folk mind. Its impact derived from the fact that, in the course of time, it coopted most of the functions of traditional social epics."

Another literary form introduced by the Spaniards which became an integral part of the local imagination was the metrical romance, which locally became the *awit* and *corrido*.[7]

"These texts were sung by local bards or read from cheap printed booklets; quotations from them were used in the duplo[8] *and their plots orally transmitted or dramatized in the* carillo *(shadowgraph) and the* komedya *or moro-moro*[9] *...It is estimated that around 200 of these romances circulated in the Philippines during the height of their popularity."*

According to Soledad Reyes,

"...The tremendous popularity of these narratives was unabated until the first quarter of the twentieth century when the novel and the short story emerged. But so close was the relationship between the awit and the prose forms that structural patterns shaping the earlier forms reappeared in the later types."

These romances range from a few hundred to several thousand lines, in stanzas of either four or five lines. Some have known authors, the most famous being Jose de la Cruz (1749 -1829) known as Huseng Sisiw, and Francisco Baltazar or Balagtas (1788-1862). Jose de la Cruz has been regarded as the first Tagalog poet of any consequence. But Francisco Baltazar is in a class by himself.

*"*Florante at Laura *was in the form of the* awit *familiar to Filipino lovers of traditional verse and it was sung like the ancient epics and the more recent* pasyon. *At the same time, it bore marks of classical learning manifest in the allusions to Greek and Roman mythology, and its figurative language was clearly patterned after the extravagant rhetoric of Spanish poetry of the Middle Ages."*

This is the story of the adventures and misadventures of the Albanian lovers, Florante and Laura, who are parted by the political intrigues of an evil member of the royal household, and are finally reunited and converted to Christianity. However, scholars now agree that the romantic trappings were a disguise for an attack against the Spanish colonial regime.

"Although the komedya *was traditionally about Christians and Moors, Balagtas chooses... to rise above*

the theme of religious war. His real concern, it would appear, is with the clash of human motives when men and women are caught up in the turmoils of social disorder." *Florante at Laura*, then, is a transitional piece, a blending of native folk narrative with European metrical romance, and of the romantic tradition with contemporary social commentary. Reyes has stressed the importance of reading this and the other romances of this period not as *"mindless entertainment"* but as attempts to create an *"alternative world, different from nineteenth century Philippines."*

Not as important as the *pasyon* but not inconsiderable in terms of quantity were the lives of saints. These narratives were anonymous and were intended as inspirational material. One of these books, *Vida: Barlaan at Josaphat,* is regarded as a forerunner of the Filipino novel. Still another type of prose narrative was the manual of conduct, like the *Urbana at Feliza* (1864) by Modesto de Castro, a native priest (the native clergy were among the first Filipino writers). Intended by its author to be an *"educational moral novel,"* it utilizes an epistolary structure to tell the story of the two sisters. It could, arguably, be considered the first Filipino novel, as it has a known author, the author being Filipino, and as its story is set in a local, contemporary setting. Narrative interest, however, has been completely subordinated to didactic purpose, namely, instruction in decorum. The characters of *Urbana at Feliza* became stereotypes familiar to later audiences of Tagalog dramas and readers of Tagalog novels.

"In perspective, Urbana at Feliza *appeared to have addressed itself to issues related to both ethics and etiquette that preoccupied most urban Filipinos... It was by projecting the ideal world populated by urbanized Filipinos that the author contained the less desirable world inhabited by those who had not fully succumbed to Hispanization and Christianization..."*

The opening of the Suez Canal in 1869 increased activity in Philippine ports. Methods of agriculture and transportation were improving. By royal decree, education up to the tertiary levels was opened to *indios.* Journalism was increasing in importance. So was book publishing. In the latter part of the 19th century, the novel-form, as it was known in Europe, was introduced into the Philippines. The new prosperity and increased leisure stimulated the taste for fiction. European novels - and later, novels written by Spaniards residing in the Philippines, set in the Philippines ("peninsular fiction") - began to be serialized in the papers.

The high point in the intellectual history of this period is the Propaganda Movement (roughly 1862-1896), to which belonged many of the men who are now honored as revolutionary heroes. These men were much influenced by the modern spirit of scientific inquiry.

They turned away from romanticism and favored empirical experience, historical realities, political problems. Most of them ended up as expatriates in Spain, either by choice or by necessity.

Philippine literature entered a new phase, acquired a national character, and became a truly "Filipino" literature, with the work of a group of men, writing and publishing mainly as expatriated in Spain in the last two decades of the 19th century."

Ironically, most of this writing was in Spanish. *Ninay* (1885), written by Pedro Paterno (1858-1911), one of the Madrid-based expatriates, can, like *Urbana at Feliza,* lay claim to being *"the first Filipino novel"* for *"it is indeed conceived as a novel by one who sees himself as a Filipino."* Unfortunately, the work has serious technical flaws, mainly its failure to integrate the melodramatic plot (Ninay, a young woman, dies of heartbreak after she is forced to part from her sweetheart, Carlos, and after both her parents die) with numerous bits of local color and sundry pieces of information on Philippine life.

The leading light of this period, and, indeed, of Philippine letters as a whole, is the man who is also revered as the national hero, Dr. Jose P. Rizal. His two novels, also written in Spanish, *Noli Me Tangere* (1887) and *El Filibusterismo* (1891), were published with great difficulty in Spain, and immediately banned by the government in Manila. Eventually, they cost their author his life.

The first novel narrates the return to his homeland of Crisostomo Ibarra, a well-born young man who has received a university education in Europe. His attempts to introduce reforms in education, believing this to be the key to social change, are foiled by two powerful Spanish friars, Padre Damaso, who turns out to be the real father of Ibarra's sweetheart, Maria Clara, and Padre Salvi, who lusts after her. He is helped by Elias, a peasant outlaw who owes Ibarra his own life. Ibarra escapes, but Elias is killed. The hapless Maria Clara seeks refuge in a convent, to escape the marriage planned for her by Damaso. The second novel is sequel to the first. Ibarra returns to Manila as Simoun, a sinister jeweler, determined to bring down the Spanish government both by corrupting the already depraved officials and friars and by assisting the native armed rebellion. He is also bent on rescuing Maria Clara from the convent, where she is defenseless against Salvi. The news that she has just died reaches Simoun on the eve of the rebellion. The rebellion fails, and Simoun is once again an embittered fugitive. But the novel ends on a quiet, tranquil note, with Padre Florentino asserting with certainty that the day will come when the people will deserve their freedom, and then, *"God provides the weapon, and the idols fall, the tyrants fall like a house of cards and liberty shines with the first dawn."*

These novels are the first works of realistic fiction to be

Tubbataha's island of birds.

produced by a Filipino. They are the work of a man steeped in both his native traditional literature as well as European literatures. They present a detailed, vivid portrait of contemporary Philippine society, as well as a searing indictment of the colonial regime. Some critics hold that they remain the most important literary works produced by a Filipino writer in any language.

"With Jose Rizal, the novel - in the European, 19th century sense of this form - can be said to have fully emerged. Though Rizal's novels were written and published on foreign soil, and shaped by impulses of a broad European tradition, they are Filipino in the particularity of motive, subject and intent. Rizal lies within a native, developing tradition. While his novels can be seen as a dramatic "qualitative leap," they can also be perceived as the natural culmination of developments in local literature prior to 1887, developments that have for some time been tending towards that synthesis of empirical and fictional impulses which these novels demonstrate."

THE AMERICAN PERIOD

Unlike the Spaniards, the American colonizers decided that it was to the advantage of the U.S. to make their language the medium of instruction in all Philippine schools.

"The University of the Philippines was founded in 1908 to train young Filipinos for tasks in the colonial bureaucracy. Its graduates and the graduates of other schools faithfully observing the mandates of American and U.S.-trained pensionado[10] *educators were to constitute a new intelligentsia that read, spoke, and wrote English. Unlike the* ilustrados[11] *of the late 19th century who belonged to the socio-economic elite, the new elite came from a broader sector of the populace. The public school system had put higher education within the reach of many Filipinos who belonged to families that were less than affluent, in a number of cases even poor. It was within the ranks of these intellectuals, whose elevated social standing was usually not matched with an equally high economic status, that Philippine writing in English had its beginnings. Although samples of writing in English had appeared as early as the first decade, only in the latter half of the 1920s did the works of Filipino writers attain the stature of literature."*

Jose Garcia Villa (1906-1997) was probably the first Filipino writer to consider himself part of the Anglo-American literary avant-garde, rather than a native writer. And his proclamation of the autonomy of art from political or moral considerations was a radical break from the tradition of writers in Tagalog and Spanish.

"After Rizal, the novel was to go through a period of vigorous existence, particularly in the native languages, a direction Rizal himself was to pursue but was unable to complete. Between Rizal's Fili *(1891) and the "first Tagalog novel" (1899) is an eight-year hiatus in which conditions became repressive and turbulent with the revolution, the collapse of the Spanish regime and the start of the American occupation."*

The writings of the Europe-based Propaganda movement had a profound influence on Philippine literature, and not just the literature written in Spanish. During the last part of the nineteenth century, the novel in Tagalog and the other Philippine languages flourished. Mojares attributes this to a number of factors: the momentum of the Propaganda Movement and the Revolution, and the awakening of racial and national awareness; the spread of secular values as a result of the collapse of Spanish rule and the influence of American occupation; the intellectual ferment created by comparative freedom in publishing, the circulation of books, and the spread of education; the emergence of a sizeable reading public with a taste for newspapers, prose fiction, and other reading fare; social changes at the turn of the century which created a climate that impelled many to write and more to read. Finally, the Spanish language was declining and the English language had not yet been fully established. This gave literature in the native languages the space it needed. The early prose fictionists had their roots in the native tradition of the *corrido, pasyon* and *duplo*. In fact, it is possible to say that the sentimental novels of the turn of the century were the descendants of the romances and books of the earlier centuries.

In matters of narrative strategies and techniques, the vernacular novels are a regression from the standard set by Rizal. This is understandable, as most vernacular novelists did not have Rizal's education or access to European literary works. Moreover, vernacular novels were mainly written for serialization in popular periodicals.

What is considered the first Tagalog novel, *Cababalaghan ni P. Bravo* was written by Gabriel Beato Francisco (1850-1935). And what is considered a *"classic traditional Tagalog novel," Ang Kasaysayan ng Magkaibigang si Nena at si Neneng* (1903), was written by Valeriano Hernandez y Peña. The latter is a direct descendant of the novel of manners, which itself descended from the nineteenth century book of manners, like *Urbana and Feliza*. The novel traces the lives of two friends who marry and undergo trials, from which one emerges triumphant and the other is defeated. The same romantic-didactic strain runs through Roman Reyes' *Pusung Walang Pag-ibig* (1910) and

Rosauro Almario's *Ang Mananayaw* and *Mga Anak-Bukid* (1911).

"...The early vernacular novels... draw from the forms of the colonial period (metrical romances, didactic narratives) as well as from the empirical types of literature favored by the times (journalistic accounts, chronicles, social tracts). Such combinations often resulted in makeshift, hybrid works."

Typical of these is Patricio Mariano's *Ang Mga Anak Dalita* (1911), which was *"a novel-in-verse, part-corrido and part-tract."* The period from 1903 to 1938 has come to be known as the *"Golden Age"* of the Vernacular Novel, but the label apparently refers more to quantity than quality. A total of 469 Tagalog novels were published. Output in the other languages was also substantial.

Reyes asserts that these early fictionists used the novel as a form of resistance. They *"sought to arrest, what in real life could not be stopped - the deepening Americanization of the Filipinos." The movement is backward-looking in its gesture of escape from contemporary life and its attendant problems and ills. Like the earlier romantic works, the novels were situated mostly in the second half of the 19th century."* This was the case with Patricio Mariano's *Tala sa Pangbulo* (1913) and the Roman Reyes' trilogy, and even with Valeriano Hernandez Peña's *Nena at Neneng* (1905), which had a contemporary setting. The conventions set by early novelists, conventions determined by what was essentially a non-realistic mode, were passed down to the next generation.

"By the third decade, this conventionalized way of perceiving reality had become a major factor in the emergence of the more "escapist" works of Fausto Galauran, Antonio Sempio, Teodoro Virrey and other novelists. Trained to treat the novels as a system of conventions - stereotyped characters, convoluted plots, inconsistent point of view, the use of rhetorical language - both the writers and the readers looked at the novels as formulas and stereotypes that did not radically differ form what had been written earlier. Although the novels usually drew on materials that could probably be verified as events in real life, the insights offered still dwelt on values centered on family life, relationships in a community and ubiquitous love relationships. The silence of these novels on matters directly related to social and economic problems sprang from many factors. But a compelling set of factors could be traced to the context of production - the outlets, the manner of distribution, editorial control, the format the serial took, and the financial arrangements between publishers and writers."

Banaag at Sikat (1905) by Lope K. Santos (1879-1963) is a "landmark" Tagalog novel in that it departs from the romantic novel of manners mode, and tackles social issues directly. But it does not quite break away from convention. Mojares calls it *"an uneasy juxtaposition of*

Giraffes roaming freely on the shores of Calauit Island.

realism and convention, making for what can perhaps be described as the 'hybrid novel'." The plot - poor boy in love with a rich girl, rich boy in love with a poor girl, with life triumphing in the end - is very much in the romantic tradition. It is also characterized by authorial intrusions, exaggerated situations, convoluted subplots, over-extended dialogue, etc. The difference is that Santos sets the action in contemporary Manila (1904) and makes the class issue central to novel. It is important also in that it *"showed subsequent authors that the social novel under the new conditions created by U.S. colonialism could focus attention on social inequities that had been sharpened by the advent of modernization."*

Faustino Aguilar's (1882-1955) *Pinaglahuan* (1907) more successfully blends the romantic plot (which again involves lovers divided by class) with political concerns (class struggle, the feudal family system, tyranny of religious beliefs, American rule, etc.). Technically, it is one of the best novels of its time.

After 1920, the novel in Tagalog became extremely commercialized. Hence the split between 'high'

and 'low' literature, and the evolution of the concept of the *bakya*[12] crowd, as opposed to the cultural elite. Reacting to this, Alejandro G. Abadilla and Clodualdo del Mundo founded *Panitikan* (literature), in 1938. At about the same time, a group of writers in English founded the Veronicans[13]. Both groups considered themselves rebels against the literary establishment. However, the tendency among Tagalog writers towards commercialization was considerably stronger than the tendency toward more serious writing, so, increasingly, the latter came to be associated with the *pambakya*, whereas Philippine writing in English came to be regarded as *pampanitikan*.

"During the early decades of the century, the lines between 'popular' and 'artistic' writing were not clearly drawn. A combination of the two was in fact aimed at by writers... Parallel to this is another significant development in the eclipse of vernacular writing. The rise of English as the language of the new intelligentsia, coupled with an education almost exclusively permeated with sajonismo (a liking for what is Anglo-Saxon), led to a cultural alienation that was to have far-reaching

effects. *The vernacular literatures dropped down the cultural scale, and almost away from the view of the new urban-oriented, university-educated generation."*

During the period immediately before World War II, writers in English in the Philippines were affected by the "proletarian literature" of the U.S.

"Jose Garcia Villa continued to be regarded with awe as some kind of literary dictator, but his "Art for Art's sake" creative philosophy was already being challenged by younger writers whose consciousness had been shaken by the social unrest around them and who had begun to look for an alternative critical orientation. The essays on letters by Salvador P. Lopez (1911-1995) later to become part of Literature and Society *(1940), offered such an alternative... Lopez's critical ideas were to serve as basis for the socially conscious "call to arms" when the Philippine Writers' League was organized in 1939."*

The debate between Villa's aestheticism and Lopez's social commitment continued into the 70s. Lumbera regards the Villa-Lopez controversy as a reflection of competing literary traditions: the Anglo-Americans vs. the Euro-Hispanic. In the Tagalog novelists Lazaro Franciso (1898-1980) and Amado Hernandez (1903-1970), who tower over novelists of the period - most of whom had succumbed to market pressures and were producing tons of sentimental novels - may be seen the vitality of the latter tradition. *Maganda Pa Ang Daigdig* (1956) and *Daluyong* (1962) by Franciso are agrarian protest novels. And *Mga Ibong Mandaragit* (1960) by Amado Hernandez is a novel of protest that picks up the story where *El Filibusterismo* left off, with a Filipino guerilla in the struggle against the Japanese finding the jewels that were thrown into the sea by Padre Florentino after the failure of the uprising against the Spaniards.

Mojares describes the difference between the Tagalog and English writers of this period as follows:

"In the case of the English writers, an apparent theoretical advancement exists side by side with a basic alienation from social realities. In the case of the Tagalog writers, a strong social predisposition is obscured and distorted by outmoded formal equipment and the lack of a large, objective historical awareness."

By the 1920s English was firmly established, both as medium of education and literary expression. Magazines like *Philippine Magazine* (1904-1941) and the *Philippines Free Press* (1908-1972), and organizations like the U.P. Writers' Club (founded in 1927 and still in existence in the eighties), the Philippine Book Guild (1936-1940) and the Philippine Writers' League (1939-1941) were attracting the most gifted literary men and women. These developments *"...sharpened the fragmentation of the audience, relegated vernacular fiction to the lower rungs of the cultural ladder, hampered the growth of the vernaculars in artistry, and alienated to a significant*

extent English writers from the popular culture."

In the 50s and early 60s, the cultural scene in Manila could have been described as a reflection of Greenwich Village, a state of affairs made possible by modern communication. Existentialism, for example, was as much a byword in Manila campuses as it was in Paris or New York. The intellectual milieu of the English writer had become much more sophisticated and cosmopolitan that that of the Tagalog writer.

Nonetheless, the early novels in English are not too different from their predecessors. For instance, the first novel in English, Zoilo Galang's (1895-1959) *A Child of Sorrow* (1921) is a simplistic and melodramatic story of thwarted love, in short, a Tagalog novel written in English. On the other hand, *The Filipino Rebel* (1927) by Maximo Kalaw (1891-1955) is a historical novel about the American conquest of the islands and the establishment of the new colonial regime, very much in the tradition of Rizal, though far less successful.

His Native Soil (1940) by Juan C. Laya (1911-1952), first-prize winner of the 1940 Commonwealth Literary Contest, is an improvement on the two earlier novels. In this return-of-the-native story,[14] Martin Romero is the idealistic reformist, Crisostomo Ibarra resurrected in Commonwealth Philippines, and, like him, he is defeated in the end.

In Mojares' view, it is with NVM Gonzalez's *Winds of April* (1940) that *"the Filipino novel takes on a definite qualitative change, manifesting the stylistic and thematic traits that have been taken to be distinctive of the English branch of Philippine fiction."* This is a first-person narrative, a kind of "impressionistic picaresque" following the journey - both physical and psychological - of a young provinciano who moves to the city. Its handling of time, its restraint, and its lyricism puts it on a different level from other novels in English.

Also interesting is the quasi-autobiographical *America Is in the Heart* (1946), written by Carlos Bulosan and published in the U.S. Bulosan was a Filipino peasant who, after graduating from high school, lived in the U.S. during the Depression years, and taught himself to write. This book is a record of the harsh life of the immigrant in America. But despite that, there are those who feel that, like *The United* (1951) by Carlos P. Romulo and like *Like a Big Brave Man* (1961) by Celso Carunungan, both of which were also published in the U.S., it *"sings the praises of America and the American."*

In the meantime, literature in Spanish was still being written; was, in fact, enjoying what Estanislao Alinea has described as a *"period of efflorescence,"* 1903 to 1942.

"The literary output was by far more voluminous at this time than in any of the previous periods... There was also an increase in the number of books printed and published,

with a greater diversification of themes. There was even a notable change in the treatment of subject-matter." Novels were both serialized in daily newspapers (*La Vanguardia, El Debate,* etc.) and printed in beautiful editions. According to Alinea, the most outstanding novelists were Antonio M. Abad and Jesus Balmori. Abad's *El campeon* was a first-prize winner in the 1940 Commonwealth Awards and *"was considered the foremost novel of the period."* It is an unusual comic novel with a fighting cock as the main character. Two of his other novels (*La oveja de Nathan* and *El ultimo romantico*) received the Premio Zobel in 1929 and 1927 respectively. Jesus Balmori's most well known novels were *Se despojo la flor* and *Los pajaros de fuego.* After the war, Spanish declined steadily. And, in the absence of translations, most Filipino students today are in complete ignorance of Philippine literature in Spanish, with the exception of Rizal, whose novels they are required to read.

THE POST-WAR NOVEL IN ENGLISH
In 1967, NVM Gonzales observed that certain themes recurred in Filipino novels in English: *The Barrio and the City* (*"it is an inevitable subject, and it has been worked out quite well. The writers of the thirties hardly knew any other"*); the Hope of the Fatherland (*"so pervasive is the influence of Rizal that we have the second inevitable theme"*); The Lost Eden (*"the best of our post-war writers took up this theme with admirable skill"*); and Now and at the Hour (*"with ampler education, a larger sophistication, and exposure to ideologies... the tension between the real and the imagined"*).

The novels about World War II, which comprise quite a number, would probably fit under the category of *"Hope of the Fatherland."* The first Filipino novel in English to deal with the nightmare of war against the Japanese is *Without Seeing the Dawn* (1947) by Stevan Javellana (1918-1977). This was followed by *Watch in the Night* (1953) by Edilberto Tiempo (1913-1996). Commenting on both novels, Bienvenido Santos wrote: *"The country's history as background for the novel gives it a scope that some novelists mistake for grandeur. Some optimistically hope it may be epical. It seems inevitable that the Filipino novel, if it must amount to anything at all, should touch on the country's history, its past, its present, and perhaps, its future. The unhappy result of all this interesting material is so much sociology and only incidentally, fictional narrative. Sometimes the result makes for fascinating history, but at other times, it is merely dull fiction."*

Ati-Atihan Festival in Kalibo, Aklan.

What should perhaps be pointed out is that in their preoccupation with history, these novelists in English are once again embracing what Lumbera has called the Euro-Hispanic tradition (as opposed to the Anglo-American tradition).

"Fortunately, there are Filipino novelists who have been more concerned with the country of the heart even as they set their story against the changing times..."

Foremost among these are Santos (1911-1996) himself, NVM Gonzales (1915 -) and Nick Joaquin (1917 -). Gonzalez is at his best when portraying *"the patient, the plodding, the faithful, the pioneer, waiting our his lease among the swampy lands in a brief season of grace." Season of Grace* (1956) draws on his earlier life in the province of Romblon and Mindoro, as do the short stories in *Children of the Ash-Covered Loam* (1954). With admirable grave and economy, it recounts the poignant story of a peasant couple and their arduous life on their remote farm, and manages to render in English the nuances and cadences of the dialect he is actually translating from. *The Bamboo Dancers* (1959), on the other hand, draws on the author's urban experiences, as do the stories in *Look, Stranger, on This Island Now* (1963), and on his expatriate years. It focuses on Ernie Rama, a Filipino pensionado, a sculptor, a middle-class intellectual, alienated and preoccupied with questions of identity. The title refers to a well-known native dance, the *tinikling,* in which the dancers must skip in and out of crashing bamboo poles, a metaphor for the clashing cultures in Philippine society.

In his first novel, *The Woman Who Had Two Navels* (1961), Nick Joaquin probes similar problems. The young heroine, Connie Escobar with her delusion about having two navels is, of course, a symbol for her generation with its twin heritage, and her meeting in Hong Kong with the disenchanted old revolutionary, Monson is a symbolic confrontation between two generations and two cultures. After they have met, the old man is able to die, and Connie is able to go on. The novel is an impressive achievement, both for its dazzling use of the English language and its mastery of narrative technique in rendering the search for a national identity. In 1965, it was described as *"by intention and execution the most ambitious long work of fiction ever attempted by a Filipino in the English language."* Though *Cave and Shadows* (1983) is structured like a mystery-thriller, it explores the same theme, drawing on a rich store of myth and legend, but locating the action in the thick of contemporary events and using a middle-class intellectual as protagonist. *"Its timeless proposition is that folk Catholicism in the Philippines, the mixture of animism and transcendent monotheism, so often belittled as spiritual mongrelization,*

may turn out to be more properly descriptive of essential spiritual-material interlocks than those imported Western doctrines which, in the past, have sometimes taught the hostile polarization of body and soul."

Joaquin has also written poems, short stories and numerous essays on Philippine history and culture. Both Gonzalez and Joaquin (like Jose Garcia Villa) have been named National Artists for Literature by the Philippine government. Bienvenido Santos would have, in all likelihood, received the same award, had he not taken American citizenship. His earlier novels - *Villa Magdalena* (1965) which is about a decaying family and class differences, *The Volcano* (1965), which is about Philippine-American relations, and *The Praying Man* (1982), which is about corruption in high places - are set in the Philippines. But his two later novels, *The Man Who (Thought He) Looked Like Robert Taylor* (1983) and *What For You Left Your Heart in San Francisco* (1987) are deeply moving portraits of the "wounded men," Filipinos in America, as are the stories he is best known for, collected in *You Lovely People* (1955), *Brother My Brother* (1960), *The Day the Dancers Came* (1967) and *The Scent of Apples* (1980).

The most important woman novelist of this post-war period is Kerima Polotan. Her *The Hand of the Enemy* (1962) has been lavishly praised for its impeccable handling of language. It is basically the story of a woman's search for love, but the search is, once again, solidly grounded in contemporary social and political realities, including a *sakdalista* movement in Pangasinan.

What comes next?

"The future of the Filipino novel in English is in the hands of those who would be bold enough and capable enough to strike new paths away from the roads that have already been long taken, who constantly live, even if in imagination only, with true tragedy, who would dedicate their life exclusively to the writing of it."

THE CONTEMPORARY NOVEL IN ENGLISH

Have they arrived, then, those young writers "bold" and "capable" enough to "strike new paths"? I believe that they have.

In 1972, Lumbera noted a hesitancy on the part of Filipino writers in English to write historical novels.[15] He speculated that this might be part of the alienation felt by these writers from the part of the national experience that antedated the literary use of English. *"One may hope that as the body of Filipino historical novels increases, our English writers' sense of alienation from the past will begin to decrease. Then the Filipino writer will ease to feel apologetic when his use of a foreign language is questioned. For, indeed there are many ways the returning native can take toward home. The use of our history opens one of them."*

In the contemporary novel in English, this "hesitancy" toward producing historical novels no longer exists, if in fact it ever did. A quick glance at the list of novels indicated (see note 1) in this paper will reveal that most of them are precisely historical novels. All of them might even be classified as "historical novels," if one were to expand the term to mean, not just novels set in periods in the remote past, but the sort of novels which Petronilo Daroy referred to in an early essay:

"In the more ambitious works, it is the nature of Philippine history and culture which the Filipino writer in English attempts to investigate."

Daroy praised Nick Joaquin for *"assimilating history into the texture of the narrative, rather than allowing it to remain a passive backdrop."*

In short, these are novels where history is not setting, but enters into the motivation of the character, propels the plot. The characters are political beings, their conflicts are engendered by political events. I would even claim that the real protagonist here is the nation itself; the real conflict, its desperate struggle for survival.

This tradition of writing, as we have seen, has always existed in the Filipino novel in all languages, and therefore cannot be regarded as a "new path." However, while it may not have been the dominant trend in the Filipino novel in English in the past,[16] today it clearly is. Contemporary novelists all go beyond the recording of the protagonists' personal conflicts, to focus on the larger problems plaguing the nation. And in this is a kind of boldness.

Most of these "historical novels" could also be called "war novels." This is hardly surprising, given that our history has been a history of a nation at war. And, since this state of chronic war makes disruption and displacement an inevitable condition, they could also be considered "novels of exile" or "exilic novels." "Exile" here admits of several meanings: expatriation and other types of dislocation, both physical and psychological, and the type of exile referred to by Dolores Feria as the *"only unifying factor in the entire body of our literature."*

"By exile, I do not mean alienation in the western sense of the word. It is something far more specific than the sense of estrangement one finds in Sherwood Anderson's grotesques, or in Conrad's cosmic orphans. It implies a historic superstructure that is uniquely Philippine, an impetus for flight and revolt which can only occur in a society in which the basic cultural components have been periodically altered by brute force."

In short, a *"chronic state of psychic exile... even if the expatriate option never confronts him."*

The difference between the expatriate characters of the earlier novels (e.g. the Bulosan and Santos characters) and those in the later novels, like Salvador de la Rza (in *Viajero*) and Johnny Manalo (in *Wings of Stone*), is that for the latter, going home is an option. The dilemma has become whether or not to stay home. Noel Bulaong (in *Killing Time in a Warm Place*) is a younger, more sophisticated version, a misfit in both province and city, in both the rebel underground and the dictatorial government, in both his own and the foreign country.

These protagonists - expatriates and non-expatriate exiles - are still in a sense, reincarnations of Rizal's Crisostomo Ibarra, perhaps an indication of both the strength of Rizal's influence on Filipino middle-class writers, and the inescapable aftermath of the historical situation that gave rise to his novels. In his study of colonialism in the Filipino novel, Jaime An Lim says:

"Ninety-six years divide the earliest novel in the group, Rizal's Noli *(1887) and the most recent, Sionil Jose's* Po-on *(1983). In spirit however, they could not have been more contemporaneous."*

Here then, over and over again, is the middle class intellectual, unable to escape his/her roots, determined to save his/her country, thwarted both by the sinister power of the enemy (in some cases still the colonial master of old, in others, his surrogate) and the tragic flaw in his/her own character, which often, as in Ibarra-Simoun, is indecision (the *Pinoy* as Hamlet?).

An interesting question might be: Will the Filipino writer of the novel in English remain an exile, unable either to accept or to change his history or his culture? I believe that the writing of the novel is in itself the beginning of change. This is true of both Filipino writers based in the Philippines and Filipino writers based abroad.

I do not wish to make a distinction between "Filipino-American writers" and "expatriate Filipino writers." Literary history/criticism in the Philippines has not been in the practice of doing so when examining the work of NVM Gonzalez, Bienvenido Santos, Carlos Bulosan or Jose Garcia Villa. Something need be said here however about the Philippine diaspora, which has certainly had an effect on Philippine letters.

Seven of the writers in my list do not live in the Philippines:[17] Linda Ty-Casper, Ceilia Manguera-Brainard, Ninotchka Rosca, Jessica Hagedorn, Eric Gamalinda, Michele Skinner and Arlene Chai. But, unlike the first generation of expatriate writers in English, these writers are not writing American immigrant novels.[18] The exception is R. Zamora Linmark, who writes about the children of *Pinoy* plantation workers in Hawaii, using their particular brand of pidgin. They are writing historical Philippine novels, something which Oscar V. Campomanes sees as a strategy for making themselves "visible," a means of coping with their exile which is different from that taken by the first generation of expatriate writers.

"The invisibility of the Philippines became a necessary historiographical phenomenon because the annexation of the Philippines proved to be constitutionally and culturally problematic for American political and civil society around the turn of the century and thereafter... For something as specific as Filipino writing in the United States, the banishment of the Philippines and Filipinos from history and the global dispersion of Filipinos, the migrant realities of Pinoy workers and urban expatriates, and the alienation of the English-speaking intellectuals from workers and peasants speaking in the vernacular must constitute a set of tangled contexts... Through a coordination of expressive tendencies and impulses of Filipino and Filipino-American writers in the U.S., a 'literature of exile and emergence' can be constructed from the normally separated realms of the old and new countries. I see the obsessive search for identity that marks Philippine literature in the colonial language (and in the vernacular...), and the identity politics articulated by the first-and-second generation Filipino-American writers... as specific streams with certain points of confluence."

For both the Fil-Am and the Filipino writers then, "home" is a coming to terms with the country, thus, an ending of the exile. Again, to cite Campomanes,

"Return for them is redefining and rewriting 'history' from the perspective of banishment... Either one is disabled... (by exile) or one is enabled, moving on... to tell the story (history) of the 'letter' (one's transcription or codification of the self-in-history) through language and the experience of one's subjection."

In their attempt to (re)write the story, contemporary Filipino novelists have appropriated a number of different strategies, ranging from those of conventional realistic fiction (as in *What For You Left Your Heart in San Francisco? The Living and the Dead*, and *Killing Time in a Warm Place*), to those generally associated with marvelous realism and post-modernism (as in *State of War, Confessions of a Volcano, The Great Philippine Jungle, Dogeaters, Empire of Memory*). They explore Philippine mythical material, an important part of the work of retrieval, of reconstruction, of re-telling of the story (in *Cave and Shadows, Song of Yvonne, The Firewalkers, State of War, The Great Philippine Jungle Energy Café*). They employ such post-modern techniques as the collage, different language registers, discontinuity of narration, etc. to depict the fragmentations and carnivalesque quality of modern Philippine life (as in *Dogeaters*). *Dogeaters*, open-ended and inconclusive as it is, seems to suggest that the

solution to the nation's problems lies in armed struggle. *Viajero* carries essentially the same message, but conveyed in a realistic style. Another realistic novel, *Wings of Stone*, though it does not actually suggest it, has an ending so violent, that only similar violence seems an adequate response.

The Honey, the Locusts, while not quite a non-realistic narrative, is a fragmented, de-centered account of war, which gives the reader the impression that he is listening to a number of tales - possibly told orally - held together only by being all about World War II, a technique that recalls Santos' in *The Man Who (Thought He) Looked Like Robert Taylor*. It offers reconciliation as a solution to recurring conflict. The message of *Song of Yvonne* is similar. The protagonist comes to understand that war is just a phase in a country's rich history, and that one must walk away from the immediate past to survive, but she also recognizes the need to recover the more distant past, the nation's roots, as they are found in the epic songs. In *Awaiting Tresspass* - which also straddles the boundary between realistic and non-realistic fiction, with its fragmented narration, time shifts, shifts in point-of-view, incursions of poetry, etc. - the wayward Telly and the priest Sevi form a strange bond, and, rejecting hatred, see what they have been blind to: the inextricable link between their individual fates, the family's fate and the country's fate.

And, though some of the novels end on an ambiguous note, with the protagonist still trapped in indecision, most - including the one comic novel in the group, *The Great Philippine Jungle Energy Café* - end on a note of affirmation.

A few novels actually conclude with a statement of what the author perceives as the role the writer must play within the postcolonial context. And what is that role? The writer must protest, he must resist his own alienation, his own marginalization. For s/he is the conscience of his race. And the writer must remember. For s/he is its memory.

These novels are steps towards retrieving the nation's fragmented past and making it whole, rewriting the story written by the conquerors that we, the conquered, and our descendants, might know it and be healed.

In Eric Gamalinda's *Empire of Memory*, Al's nephew, Nico, announces that he has decided to stay in the country despite his being an American citizen, and that he may someday write a book about it. And Al says: " *'It's a very good thing to do,' I tell him. A lot of people are escaping, fleeing on fragile boats. The young man wants to stay."*

In F. Sionil Jose's *Viajero*, the dying Salvador de la Raza says:

"It is they who will redeem Filipinas, bestow on her the honor that was squandered, the future that was betrayed by the demons of colonialism and the cupidity of her own native sons. All this is now here, engraved not just in my mind but in the record, incomplete though it may be, their forbearance."

And in Ninotchka Rosca's *State of War*, Anna muses: *"And she knew instantly. She was pregnant, the child was male, and he would be born here, with the* labuyo - *consort of mediums and priestesses - in attendance. He would be nurtured as much by her milk as by the archipelago's legend - already, she was tucking Guevarra's voice among the other voices in her mind - and he would be the first of the Capuchin monk's descendants to be born innocent, without fate... She knew all that instantly, with great certainty, just as she knew that her son would be a great storyteller, in the tradition of the children of priestess. He would remember, his name being a history unto itself, for he would be known as Ismael Villaverde Banyaga."*

Our historians have begun this reexamination and reinterpretation of our long, complex colonial history, as well as our more recent history under the Marcos dictatorship. The contribution of the novelists - in English, yes, and in Filipino and the other Philippine languages certainly - is that they are doing it through imaginative reconstruction. And in this they are simply being absolutely true to tradition.

Tubbataha's island of birds.

---

* FOOTNOTES

1 - I came up with thirty-nine titles: Bienvenido Santos' "The Man Who (thought He) Looked Like Robert Taylor" (1983), Nick Joaquin's "Caves and Shadows" (1983), F. Sionil Jose's "Mass" (1983), Alfredo Salanga's "The Birthing of Hannibal Valdez" (1984), Edilberto Tiempo's "The Cracked Mirror" (1984), F. Sionil Jose's "Poon" (1984), Linda Ty Casper's "Fortress in the Plaza" (1985), Edilberto Tiempo's "The Standard Bearer" (1985), Bienvenido Santos' "Villa Magdalena" (1986), Bienvenido Santos' "What the Hell For You Left Your Heart in San Francisco?" (1987), Linda Ty Casper's "Ten Thousand Seeds" (1987), Ninotchka Rosca's "State of War" (1987) and "Twice Blessed" (1988), Alfred Yuson's "The Great Philippine Jungle Energy Café" (1988), Linda Ty Casper's "A Small Party in a Garden", (1988), F. Sionil Jose's "Ermita" (1988), Linda Ty Casper's "Awaiting Trespass" (1989), Eric Gamalinda's "Planet Waves" (1989) and "Confessions of a Volcano" (1990), Carmen Guerrero Nakpil's "The Rice Conspiracy" (1990), Azucena Grajo Uranza's "Bamboo in the Wind" (1990), Jessica Hagedorn's "Dogeaters" (1990), Linda Ty Casper's "Wings of Stone" (1990), Cecilia Manguera Brainard's "Song of Yvonne" (1991), Jose V. Dalisay Jr.'s "Killing Time in a Warm Place" (1992), Erwin Castillo's "The Firewalkers" (1992), Eric Gamalinda's "Empire of Memory" (1992), Lina Espina Moore's "The Honey, The Locusts" (1992), Edith Tiempo's "The Alien Corn" (1992), E. Vallado Daroy's "Hazards of Distance" (1992), F. Sionil Jose's "Viajero" (1992), Antonio Enriquez's "The Living and the Dead" (1994), Edith Tiempo's "One, Tilting Leaves" (1995), R. Zamora Linmark's "Rolling the R's" (1995), Michele Skinner's "Mango Seasons" (1996), Cristina Pantoja Hidalgo's "Recuerdo" (1996), Arlene Chai's

"The Last Time I Saw Mother" (1996), Renato Madrid's "Devil Wings" (1996), and Linda Ty Casper's "Dream Eden" (1996).

2 - Tagalog is the language of the national capital region, and became the basis for Filipino, the national language of the Philippines.

3 - The brightest achievement of Philippine writing in English belongs to the postwar period. By 1940, however, the basic lineaments of this literature had already emerged. (Mojares 1983:351)

4 - In his study of the Filipino epics, Angalito Santos says that he was unable to retrieve a single authenticated text retrieved before 1880. "Though none of these texts can definitely be said to be pre-Hispanic, they are patently non-colonial discourses. It is, of course, axiomatic that they constitute the highest literary-cultural expression of the more than 120 cultural communities which today make up the Filipino people. (Santos 1997:105)

5 - The sinakulo or cenaculo is a stage play on the passion and death of Christ, performed during the Lenten season, like the pasyon.

6 - Ileto writes: "Authorship is irrelevant in the case of the Pasyon Pilapil because it bears the stamp of popular consciousness...It is beyond doubt that a text like Pasyon Pilapil was, for all purposes, the social epic of the nineteenth century Tagalogs and probably other lowland groups as well."

7 - The awit and the corrido differ from each other in type of versification.

8 - The duplo is the traditional art of poetic jousting, a debate carried on in improvised verse.

9 - The komedya borrowed its plot from medieval Spanish ballads about noble warriors and their adventures, but transformed these adventures into battles between Christian soldiers and Moslem rebels in the Philippines.

10 - The pensionados were the first group of Filipinos to be sent by the American colonial government to the U.S. on scholarships.

11 - The term ilustrado refers to the native elite, many of them mestizo Spanish or mestizo Chinese.

12 - Bakya refers to wooden clogs, which in the popular imagination is associated with the lower classes, who were not in the habit of wearing shoes.

13 - The Veronicans were so named because of Veronica Press where they published their Story Manuscripts.

14 - The American scholar, Gerald Burns, has written an interesting study of the "repatriate theme" in Philippine literature. See "The Repatriate Theme in Philippine Second-Language Fiction" (Burns 1992).

15 - An obviously different observation from Bienvenido Santos. See above.

16 - Consider, for instance, A Lion in the House by Lina Espina Moore (1980), which might be called a "domestic novel", dealing with marital infidelity; Blade of Fern by Edith Tiempo (1978) which deals with a disillusioned young man's flight from the city and his regeneration in a little mining town.

17 - I shall not include Bienvenido Santos, who returned to Manila, and passed away in 1996.

18 - However, Jessica Hagedorn's second novel, Gangster of Love (1996), is about Asian-American artists and rock musicians in New York. I have not included it in my list of Filipino novels.

A brief history of Philippine architecture

by Bernardo M. Perez

Bernardo M. Perez, OSB has earned his BS degree in Architecture from the University of Santo Tomas. He is the current rector of San Beda College. Some of his works are: "Folk Architecture" which he co-authored with Rosario Encarnacion and Julian Dacanay, and "Arkitektura", an essay on Philippine architecture that was made into a documentary video. He was awarded a Doctorate in Humane Letters (Honoris Causa) and Patnubay ng Sining at Kalinangan ñ Panitikan.

Above
Church interior on the island of Bohol.

Photo facing the title page
Detail of a Torogan, the ancestral home
of the sultans of Marawi City, Mindanao.

The history of Philippine architecture may be divided into three periods: the precolonial, the Spanish colonial, and the American colonial and contemporary periods. The first begins in the prehistoric era and ends in 1565; the second covers the years 1565 to 1898, and the third coincides with the twentieth century. There are no written records on architecture before 1565, and no existing building dates back to that period. However, many indigenous communities build their houses following a tradition that must have originated in that era.

The earliest shelters were caves. Archaeological evidence shows that the Tabon caves on the western coast of the island of Palawan were inhabited about thirty thousand years ago. Nomadic people in the Philippines still live in the lean-to, a screen with a frame of tree branches or twigs with leaves as the siding. A report written in 1583 mentioned houses built on trees. In 1969, archaeologists found tree post-holes of houses built about three to five thousand years ago. These were square, one-room dwellings on ground level.

Existing ethnic houses are one-room dwellings, raised on stilts, and covered by a steep thatched roof. The posts are of wood, and the sidings are of either wood, bamboo or thatch. The number of posts varies, from four to more than forty. The roof may be gabled, pyramidal, or hipped. Some roofs combine the four-sloped hip roof with a steeper two-slope gabled roof.

The more notable houses are those of the peoples of the mountainous Cordillera and those of the Muslims in Mindanao. The sea-faring, coastal peoples build their houses on stilts over the water. The torogan or chief's house of the Maranao has protruding beam ends which are intricately carved, and massive posts which rest on round stones over the ground for protection against earthquakes.

The *bahay kubo*, the bamboo and thatch house of the lowlands, is one type of ethnic dwelling. It is found with many variations throughout the islands. The floors made of slightly separated bamboo slats allow cool air to rise into the interior. One feature of the house is the *batalan* or unroofed porch with a floor of bamboo slats.

162

When the Spaniards established settlements in 1565, they lived in houses similar to those of the natives. Even the cathedral and churches of Manila were made of wood, bamboo and thatch. In 1583, the city was consumed by fire. With the discovery of volcanic tuff deposits near the city, churches, government buildings, houses and the wall around Manila were made of stone. However, all these were destroyed by the earthquake of 1645. As a result, houses were built with a wooden frame and stone walls. This more flexible construction, called arquitectura mestiza or mixed architecture, had a better chance of surviving tremors.

The friars who evangelized the peoples in the countryside reorganized the villages and established towns following the ordinances issued by King Philip II in 1573. The center of the town was the plaza around which streets were laid out in a grid iron pattern.

The church was the most prominent building in the town. The early churches were made of wood, bamboo and thatch. They were later expanded and made of stone or brick, and were strengthened with buttresses that insured their stability during earthquakes. The simple, rugged style had been called "earthquake baroque." On one side of the church, or away from it, stood the belltower, and on the other was the convento. The façade and the side portal of the church were decorated. Various styles of ornaments were used in both exterior and interior: renaissance, baroque, rococo, and neoclassic. The native workmen interpreted the design of the ornaments according to their skill, temperament and taste, and would even introduce local motifs, such as flowers and foliage. This resulted in a baroque or rococo that was more Filipino than European. Most of the churches were built in the seventeenth and eighteenth centuries.

From the *bahay kubo* developed the *bahay na bato*, the house of wood and stone, similar to *arquitectura mestiza*. The house had two stories: the living quarters

On the next page
Tagbilaran Church.
Below
Convent on Siquijor Island in the Visayas.

were on the upper floor whereas the lower level, largely vacant, was used for storage. The frame, flooring as well as the second-story sidings were made of wood; a stone wall surrounded the ground floor; and the roof was either of tile or thatch.

Unlike the *bahay kubo*, the *bahay na bato* was large and spacious and had many rooms. It had an elaborate system of windows. The large upper window had two sets of sliding shutters - one with *capiz* (oyster shells) or glass panes, the other with wooden louvers or jalousies. The lower window, which was from floor level to about waist height, had sliding wooden shutters. The opening was protected by a wooden balustrade or an iron grill. Intricate woodcarvings decorated the interior of the house. Doors, transoms, arches, fretwork panels running above partitions, and the balustrades of stairs were all works of art. At the back of the house was the azotea, a terrace on the level of the second floor. Under it was a cistern where rainwater from the roof was stored. The *bahay na bato*, a stately tropical house, reached its full development in the late nineteenth century.

In the first five years of the Americans' presence in the country, the biggest building constructed was an ice plant. It was likewise inevitable that one project given top priority was the establishment of a summer capital in a cool region 250 kilometers north of Manila, and 1,500 meters above sea level. The American architect Daniel H. Burnham prepared development plans for both Baguio and Manila, and chose William E. Parsons to implement them. Parsons had studied at Yale, Columbia and the Ecole des Beaux Arts in Paris.

Aside from preparing plans for urban development, Parsons designed school and government buildings, the Philippine General Hospital, the Manila Hotel, clubhouses, and markets. His buildings - the first reinforced concrete structures in the country - were simple, straightforward, and functional. They were the primary examples of modern architecture in the Philippines.

After Parsons' departure in 1914, Filipino architects who had been trained in the United States and Europe began to dominate the scene. Among them was Juan Arellano, who designed the Legislative Building and the Post Office Building in the neo-classic style, and the Metropolitan Theatre which was of art deco. Juan Nakpil, who had studied in the United States and France, joined the firm of Andres Luna de San Pedro who had studied and worked in Paris. Together they designed some notable structures such as the Perez-Samanillo Building. Luna designed the Crystal Arcade, which, before World War II, was considered the most modern edifice in the Philippines. Another significant

artist of the time was Pablo Antonio, who was also influenced by art deco. He is given credit for the Far Eastern University Main Building and the Ramon Roces Publications Building.

Post-war Filipino architects who had studied in the United States - Carlos Arguelles, Angel Nakpil, and Cesar Concio - were influenced by the International Style. The buildings of that period employed sunbreaks or *brise-soleil*, a device apppropriate for the tropics.

Modern architecture in the Philippines went into a romantic phase in the works of Leandro Locsin and Gabriel Formoso. Locsin designed the Cultural Center of the Philippines and several five-star hotels. Formoso's works included the Asian Institute Management (AIM) Building and the Pacific Star Building. Another fine example of romanticism was the San Miguel Corporation Head Office designed by Jose Mañosa. The earliest instance of French influence on Philippine architecture was in the late eighteenth century when rococo as a decorative style appeared in church art. The rococo period in Europe began in 1715 and ended in 1790 whereas, in the Philippines, it began in 1780 and lasted until 1817. Was the introduction of rococo in the country a result of the Bourbon revival in Spain and of the direct voyages from Spain to the Philippines since 1765? Some fine examples of this style are the façades of the Churches of Tanay, Argao and Miag-ao as well as the retablos of Tanay, Argao and Betis.

In the early decades of the twentieth century, Filipino architects studied in American schools influenced by the Ecole des Beaux Arts. For this reason, government buildings designed between 1913 and1941 were in the neo-classic or neo-renaissance style. Provincial capitols and public school buildings throughout the islands are the legacy of that period.

In 1925, Juan Nakpil visited the Art Deco Exposition in Paris. Upon his return to the Philippines, he became an exponent of the style. While government structures were in the neo-classic style, commercial buildings, particularly moviehouses, proclaimed the new age of art deco.

As art deco became the fashion of the twenties and thirties, so did the brise-soleil become the rage in the fifties and sixties. These were inspired by the Ministry of Education and Health Building in Rio de Janeiro designed by Lucio Costa and Oscar Niemeyer, with Le Corbusier as consultant and whose designs used sunbreaks. Although French influences on the country's architectural style were indirect because these came through Spain, the United States and Brazil, and through Filipinos who had been in France, they were nevertheless decisive in the development of twentieth century Philippine architecture.

Philippine art
and cinema

by Patrick Flores

PATRICK FLORES is the Chairperson of the Department of Art Studies, College of Arts and Letters, University of the Philippines at Diliman. He has an undergraduate degree in Humanities and an MA in Art History, and is currently pursuing his doctorate in Philippine film studies. He is the founding member of the Film Desk of the Young Critics Circle.

As mirrors and seers of its history, the arts and cinema of the Philippines capture images of conflict and change. In the course of time and across spaces, the experience of a people and a culture collect its most vital expression in forms which ceaselessly conceive identities and give justice to the tradition and turbulence of a life of transformation.

Attentively observing the recent work of Philippine artist Gaston Damag, a Paris resident, we discern the kind of sensibility that imbues artistic choices which contemporary Filipino artists - either at home or abroad - avail of today. In a three-part display, the artist tortures the *bulol,* the wooden sculpture of the rice granary god of the northern peoples of the Cordilleras, by cutting it up and pinning it down. Several corroded I-beams fasten the idol to the floor as fluorescent light illuminates the locus of burden. In another site of wreckage, the sculpture is dismembered beyond recognition under the gaze of an incandescent bulb. Is this sacrilege necessary to regain our identity across the discrepant contexts of indigenous, folk, Muslim, modern, and contemporary cultures ?

Damag's art signifies the current concern among Philippine artists to explore possibilities in the field of themes, materials, discourses and styles. Conventional modes of making art have failed to address urgent issues and debates on identity, political engagement and moral accountability. Many young artists have learned, with wonder and curiosity, to come to grips with hybrid forms like installation, performance art, mixed media, collage, assemblage, and diverse forms of site-specific works. In this pursuit, they need not look far for inspiration. Philippine art and culture have always held out manifold and munificent options as far as a kind of expression that touches base with feeling, thought, and action is concerned: the Maytime festival of house decorations in Lucban, the Lenten practices of self-flagellation, and even the veneration of saints on altars engage all the senses of the body in the encounter with art.

Long before Spanish colonizers would conquer the islands and gain a vineyard of souls and spices, the archipelago had nourished a lively native civilization, largely sustained by indigenous mythology, a strong Islamic presence in the south, and thriving trade relations with Southeast Asian empires. Traditions in textile, pottery, metalware, jewelry, personal adornment, ceramics, and other practices made possible by maritime exchange were collective endeavors, never divorced from commitments to daily life. Oral literature in the form of epic poetry and other narratives wove tales of birth, the origin of the cosmos, and the hereafter.

The performing arts were equally vibrant as rituals, dance, and music pervaded the lives of the country's varied peoples. And architecture, with some structures appearing and feeling like wombs, did not only withstand the onslaught of the hostile elements, but also aspired to touch the skies: the Ifugao rice terraces testify to life-giving engineering and the grains of the earth flowing from the wellspring of nurtured nature, while the panolong which distinctly marks the Muslim house looks like a boat's prow, sailing like a royal barge. Colonialism would alter the cultural course of the islands altogether. As a condition of force, it sought to create new identities among its subjects and ordain a future that was to end in revolution.

The range of the colonial arts revolved around the church and its daily activities, from processions to masses, from prayers to feasts of saints, from Christmas to Good Friday. The indigenous matrix of culture soon gave way to Catholic doctrine and European norms, with the locus of expression relocated from the fields to the folds of the colonial town. Suddenly, some forms spiritually dear to the people took on derogatory dimensions, and soon aesthetic experience came under the close surveillance of colonial structures. Consequently, hierarchies rose among natives from whose own ranks an elite emerged. They built houses of stone and received guests in dwellings reminiscent of the humble nipa house on stilts, now adorned with the accoutrements of newfound prestige and wealth. In Intramuros, the Walled City of colonial Philippines, imposing religious and civil structures rose ; and even in the remotest town, a Catholic church stood even if solitarily, serving as temple and military outpost.

On the brink of the revolution at the turn of the century, as the Philippines opened its harbors to free trade, aesthetic tutelage reached its peak, with Juan Luna and Felix Resurreccion Hidalgo winning Gold and Silver prizes at the Madrid Exposition of 1884. Several decades earlier, the Academia de Dibujo, one of the earliest formal schools of painting on the islands, was founded by a native maestro named Damian Domingo. This shining moment of colonial achievement in Spain was, however, also to be the colony's undoing.

Juan Luna embodied the ideals of the Enlightenment and was an ilustrado, a member of the community of bright Philippine patriots who studied in Europe and imbibed the libertarian ideals of the time. Philippine National Hero Jose Rizal was at the helm of the struggle for reform in the Philippines.

Two days after Jose Rizal was shot at Bagumbayan and as the Katipunan swept the land with the fervor of war, the first films to come to the Philippines had begun to unreel in a small projection house in downtown Escolta, Manila. Showing short documentaries of banal scenes from the Gaumont Chronophotograph, the Salon Pertierra theater opened to eager audiences. This was rather a precocious film historical event in a local

Photo facing the title page
Juan Luna. "Study for Rice Harvesting" detail .
below
1 Fernando C. Amorsolo "Coming Home from the Farm" 1949.
2 Felix Ressureccion Hidalgo "Don Perez de Dasmarinas" 1896.
3 Victorio Edades "The Sketch" 1928.

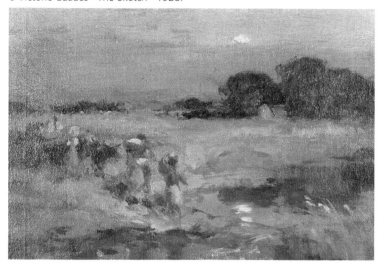

1

2

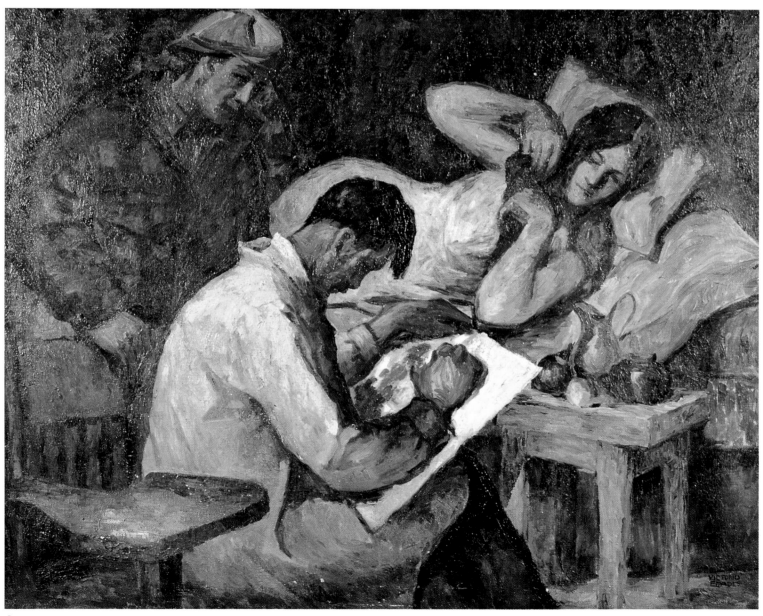

3

setting many miles away from the center, considering that it was only three years before that the copyright of Edison's commercial films was awarded. Two years later, Filipino businessman Antonio Ramos brought in Lumiere's cinematograph, and showed films at #31 Escolta under the auspices of Swiss merchants Leibman and Peritz.

The emergence of cinema in the country resonated with the founding of the nation, thus rendering silver and sterling the revolutions of 1896 and 1898.

In the wake of America's victory in the Pacific, the cinema entrenched itself in the islands as colonial technology. Ethnographic films were made about the Philippines. These films did not so much describe the Philippines as project a sense of progress in the hands of American rulers. It was also at that time that three significant aspects of filmmaking would take root: censorship, the imposition of government taxes, and international distribution.

With a new dedicated public setting into place, mainly in Manila and Cebu in the Visayas, and watching movies becoming a way of life, an industry which would cater to the new taste had to rise. This industry was to be patterned after the scheme hatched in the minds of Hollywood's forebears. The first Filipino film was shown in 1919. Jose Nepomuceno's `Dalagang Bukid (Country Girl) was a *zarzuela*, a song and dance form, featuring the period's star of the theater, Honorata de la Rama; she would sing the theme song live every screening. The earliest film people came from *zarzuela* companies; one of them, Vicente Salumbides, worked as a movie extra in Hollywood.

The colonial theater context against which the early stages of Philippine cinema emerged is important in connecting film to the previous artistic habits of staging reality and showing it to the public. Colonial theater, from the Passion of Christ to the mock battle between Moors and Christians, arose from feudal conditions, but also intimated subversion from within the tradition as gleaned from the passionate politics of the seditious *zarzuelas* in the American period.

The Japanese Occupation made the industry realize that cinema as a social institution packs power, construed by the State as a potent medium which must be reined in through censorship and unleashed through propaganda. The Japanese clamped down on movie production and put in place strict guidelines for censorship. After the war, the guerrilla-garrison genre came to the fore, a narrative built around Japanese atrocities and the celebration of Yankee liberation and guerrilla struggle. Soon, however, as the industry moved on to post-war reconstruction, it would be gripped by nostalgia for nation, a sense of mourning for things lost in war. Such bereavement seems to have sharpened the creative

instincts of filmmakers. The First Golden Age of Philip-pine Movies flew on the wings of such post-war ambivalence.

It was also nostalgia laced with tourism and commerce that the Philippine painter Fernando Amorsolo captured how the sunlight fell on the bodies and surfaces of the local domain. The Master was so popular that he ordained a tradition of conservatism for almost three decades, a virtual stranglehold which would only be challenged by Victorio Edades who upon return from the United States in the twenties introduced certain ideas about distortion; the latter did not sit well with Amorsolo's pleasant pictorial compositions. The Edades experiments and the ensuing debates on modernism blazed the trail for the Philippine modern movement which found its acme in the sixties with the flourishing of the Abstract school, both of the gestural and geometric tendencies, and the remarkable translation of Western idioms into local expression.

When the studio system collapsed in the late fifties, the Philippine film industry groped for direction. In the absence of a system which coordinated a program of sound film entertainment fare, ersatz versions of film trends abroad flooded the local market: spaghetti westerns, detective films, sex flicks, martial arts pictures, and so on. As part of the tactics of fly-by-night producers who had simply wanted to recoup investment after exhibition, these films lost sight of the heritage of the past and exploited the audience's fascination with Hollywood and its Third World imitations. It was also during this time when the soft-core genre, called bomba (bomb in literal terms), gained auspice as Martial Law's dominant cinematic aesthetic.

At the dark heart of the seventies was Ferdinand Marcos's dictatorship which plunged the nation into the terror of authoritarian rule. Against such repression, however, sprung both contradictions and continuities: Nora Aunor, the industry's biggest star and greatest performer, practically roused mass hysteria with her rags-to-riches myth, teenage blockbusters, and immense talent. At the height of her stardom, she significantly shifted gears, starring in movies by filmmakers who espoused social realist aesthetics and New Wave technical innovations. Lino Brocka, Ishmael Bernal and Miguel De Leon are the most well-known exemplars.

The late Brocka, for instance, broke new ground when his films were invited to the prestigious Cannes International Film Festival. He even once served as member of the jury in the eighties, and continues to be regarded as one of the leading lights of Third World filmmaking.

The stirrings of social realism in an era marked by decadence and dissent defined the seventies, which saw the almost contemporaneous emergence of

Juan Luna "Study for Rice Harvesting" 1895.

social realism and conceptual art. The latter was coddled by the Cultural Center of the Philippines through the First Lady's program of culture which promoted internationalism, the avant garde, and the whole gamut of cosmopolitan forms from ballet to classical music and murals. The monolithic cantilevered structure of the Cultural Center of the Philippines was the nervecenter and symbol of Imelda's grandiose ambitions; it was also designed as the country's bid for international recognition. An architectural style inspired by internationalist trends, Leandro Locsin's masterpiece shaped the aesthetic of Imelda's edifice complex: the Folk Arts Theater, the Philippine International Convention Center, and later the Film Center - all standing on land reclaimed from the historic Manila Bay, from which the main roads of American colonial Manila had radiated as planned by the architect Daniel Hudson Burnham who imagined the city as a hub of neo-classical office buildings and art deco structures.

The complex social situation presenting itself after the uprising which toppled the Marcos government in 1986

threw the more progressive filmmakers off track. The conditions were now different, the enemy was no longer the dictator, and a new aesthetic had to be ushered in to define the feeling for the times. The Aquino administration did not help much, relegating culture to the lowest rung of its priorities even as it democratized access to the Cultural Center of the Philippines's cultural dissemination.

The present dispensation of President Fidel V. Ramos has appropriated art and culture as instruments of global competitiveness and the main resources for staging the rituals of the centennial celebrations.

As Philippine art recalls to mind and heart the memory of revolution, it awaits its own through the search of identity in a season of diaspora, a quest for questions that hopes to finally cut against the grain - against the lines of destiny and destination - divined by its very nation.

"*Rizal*"

Translated from the French
by Eileen Powis

The exemplary life and tragic destiny of Jose P. Rizal (1861-1896) bear witness to this great Filipino figure's total commitment in the battle for freedom. His enormous talent as a writer permitted him to carry on the struggle for the liberation of his country and made him a national hero glorified by his people. This charismatic leader from a generation of intellectuals moulded by the ideas of the French Revolution, whom Unamuno compared to Hamlet, Don Quixote and Christ, has left us two acknowledged masterpieces from a prematurely interrupted body of literary creation: *Noli MeTangere* and *El Filibusterismo.*

Rizal thus remains, within the great emancipatory movement that stirred up Asia during the 20th century and which continues to drive Latin America and Africa today, a link and a vital reference for those who continue to struggle for the rights of man, justice and peace.

His intellectual and moral qualities, the international prestige of his prophetic thinking - was he not a pro-European ahead of his time? - the serenity of his sacrifice, allowed him to incarnate this independence whose centennial the Republic of the Philippines is celebrating.

In this framework and in homage to this emblematic figure, a film devoted to his life is being produced in the Philippines. This initiative, supported by the Centennial Commission, as was also the case for this book, should permit the universal values to which the Filipino people are attached to be spread through the telling of his story.

We have wished to cultivate this symbol by presenting a few images from "Rizal" (GMA Films, Inc.).

Cesar Montano as Rizal..

Acknowledgements

The editors would like to thank all those, French and Filipino alike, who have given their advice and assistance:

Sec. Mina T. Gabor, Department of Tourism, Republic of the Philippines
Ms. Jazmin C. Esguerra, Tourism Attache, Philippine Embassy in Paris
Mr. Samuel le Caruyer de Beauvais, French Ambassador to the Philippines
Mr. Marcel Jouve, Cultural Attache, French Embassy in the Philippines
Mr. Renaud Fessaguet, Director, Alliance Française de Manille
National Artist Nick Joaquin
Mr. Jean-Claude Masson
Mr. Luis Morales, Director, National Centennial Commission
Mrs. Carmen Pedrosa, Member, National Centennial Commission
Mr. Ramon A. Recto,President, Supply Oilfield Sevices, Inc.
GMA/FILMEX, the production company for the film, "Rizal"; Marilou Diaz Abaya,
director; Jimmy Duavit and Butch Jimenez, producers; Denni Tan, make-up artist
stylist and Mike Guison, costume designer
The actors in the film "Rizal", Ms. Chin-Chin Gutierrez and Mr. Cesar Montano
Father Gabriel Casal, Director, Philippine National Museum
Mr. Philippe Gauthier, Asiatype
Mr. Gerard Lanfrey, Director, Air France (Manila)
Mr. Ibarra Gonzalez, for his literary participation
Ms. Romina L. Santos, for the editorial coordination (Manila-Paris)
Mss. Renedel C. Vidanes, Cherry Corsame, Mary Ann Nieto
and Chinqui Roldan, S.O.S. Chairman's Office
Mr. Senen Lazaro, VP Operations, S.O.S. Inc. (Coordination U.P.-S.O.S., Inc.)
Mrs. Cynthia Heussaff

Photo Credits

© The photographs published in this book are under the copyright of Eric Pasquier
    and le cherche midi éditeur except for the following:
    page 143: Photo Cormier
    pages 166, 169, 171: Philippine National Museum - Jimmy D. Oblena, Photographe
    pages 160, 162-164: Photo Bernardo M. Perez, OSB

Editor: Louis Aldebert

Graphic Designer: Alain Cianci

Copyright©1998 cherche midi éditeur - Paris
© Andres Cristobal Cruz for the English translation
    by Nick Joaquin of Jose P. Rizal's poem "Mi Ultimo Adios"

Table of contents

ISBN 2 862 7459 60

Impression et reliure : Pollina s.a., 85400 Luçon - n° 74831-A

Dépôt légal : juin 1998

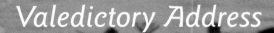

Valedictory Address

Land that I love - farewell! O land the Sun loves!
Pearl in the sea of the Orient: Eden lost to your brood!
Gaily go I to present you this hapless hopeless life;
were it more brilliant, had it more freshness, more bloom;
still for you would I give it - would give it for your good.

In barricades embattled, fighting with delirium,
others donate you their lives without doubts, without gloom,
The site doesn't matter: cypress, laurel or lily,
gibbet or open field, combat or cruel martyrdom,
are equal if demanded by country and home.

I am to die when I see the heavens go vivid,
announcing the day at last behind the dead night.
If you need colour, colour to stain that dawn with
let spill my blood, scatter it in good hour,
and drench in its gold one beam of the newborn light.

My dreams when a lad, when scarcely adolescent;
my dreams when a young man, now with vigour inflamed;
were to behold you one day - Jewel of eastern waters!
griefless the dusky eyes; lofty the upright brow,
unclouded, unfurrowed, unblemished and unashamed!

Enchantment of my life, my ardent avid obsession:
To your health! cries the soul, so soon to take the last leap;
To your health! O lovely, how lovely, to fall that you may rise!
to perish that you may live! to die beneath your skies!
and upon your enchanted ground the eternities to sleep!

Should you find someday, somewhere on my gravemound,
fluttering among tall grasses, a flower of simple fame;
caress it with your lips and you kiss my soul.
I shall feel on my face across the cold tombstone,
of your tenderness: the breath - of your breath: the flame.

Suffer the moon to keep watch, tranquil and suave, over me;
suffer the dawn its flying lights to release;
suffer the wind to lament in murmurous and grave manner;
and should a bird drift down and alight on my cross,
suffer the bird to intone its canticle of peace.